Dec 2017

Dad,
For your enjoyment
thinking of your time
in Panama!
Love,
Claire & Don

A History of Panama and its Development

Farnham Bishop

A History of Panama and its Development

LM Publishers

CHAPTER I[1]

GEOGRAPHICAL INTRODUCTION

A hundred thousand years ago, when the Gulf of Mexico extended up the Mississippi Valley to the mouth of the Ohio, and the ice-sheet covered New York, there was no need of digging a Panama Canal, for there was no Isthmus of Panama. Instead, a broad strait separated South and Central America, and connected the Atlantic and Pacific oceans. This was the strait that the early European navigators were to hunt for in vain, for long before their time it had been filled up, mainly by the lava and ashes poured into it by the volcanoes on its banks.

But though the formation of the Isthmus is for the most part volcanic, it has very few volcanoes of its own, and all of these have been extinct for untold centuries. The so-called volcano in the Gaillard Cut, about which so much was once said in the American newspapers, was nothing but a small mass of rock that had become heated in a curious and interesting way. The intense heat of the sun— thermometers have registered a hundred and twenty degrees in certain parts of the Cut at noon—caused the spontaneous combustion of a deposit of sulphur

---

[1] This book was originally published in 1913 under the title *Panama: past and present.*

7

and iron pyrites or "fool's gold." The smoldering sulphur heated a small pocket of soft coal, which in turn produced heat enough to crack holes in the rock, out of which came blue sulphur smoke and steam from rain water that had dropped on this natural stove. Except that care had to be taken in planting charges of dynamite in drill-holes near by, this toy volcano had no effect whatever on the canal work, and was presently dug up by a steam-shovel, and carried away on flat-cars.

Volcanic eruptions are unknown on the Isthmus of Panama, and earthquakes are very rare. The great earthquake that devastated the neighboring republic of Costa Rica in 1910, barely rattled the windows in Panama. The last shock of any severity was felt there in 1882, when considerable damage was done to the cathedral, and to the Panama Railroad, and the inhabitants were very badly frightened. But for more than two hundred years there has been no earthquake strong enough to bring down the famous "flat arch" in the church of San Domingo, in the city of Panama. This arch, which was built at the end of the seventeenth century, has a span of over forty feet and a rise of barely two, and all the engineers that have seen it agree that only a little shaking would be needed to make it fall.

Geographically, Panama is the connecting link between South and Central America. Politically, it lies between the republic of Costa Rica and the United States of Colombia, of which it was once a part. It is a much larger country than most people realize, having a length of four hundred and twenty-five miles, and a width of from thirty-one to one hundred and eighteen miles, with an area of about thirty-three thousand, five hundred square miles, which is very nearly the size of the State of Maine. At the place where the canal is being built, the Isthmus is about forty miles wide, but though the actual distance from ocean to ocean is less in other places, the only break in the central range of mountains, the Cordilleras del Bando, that runs from one end of the country to the other, occurs at this point. At the narrowest part of the Isthmus, near the South American end, the hills are from one to two thousand feet high, while near the Central American end there are not a few peaks of from six to seven thousand feet. At the summit of the old pass at Culebra, before the engineers began to cut it down, the continental divide was only two hundred and ninety feet above sea-level.

On either side of the Cordilleras, broad stretches of jungle or open prairie slope down to the sea, the former predominating on the Atlantic side, the latter on the Pacific. Numerous streams flow into the two oceans. The largest of these is the Tuyra, which, with its tributary, the Chucunaque, empties into the Gulf of San Miguel, near the spot where Balboa waded into the Pacific (see page 61). The second largest and the best known of the rivers of Panama is the famous Chagres, whose mouth is only six miles from the Atlantic entrance of the canal. Like the Tuyra and the Chepo on the Pacific side, the Chagres is navigable for large canoes and small launches for many miles, particularly in the rainy season. River communication is very important in a heavily wooded country where roads are scarce and bad, as they were in the United States before the Revolution, and are still on the Isthmus today. Though most of the smaller streams are little more than creeks, they produce a great volume of water-power which may some day be utilized.

There are no lakes of any size, but there are several lagoons or natural harbors, almost completely landlocked. Chiriqui Lagoon, on the Atlantic near the Costa Rica line, has long been used as a coaling station by the United States Navy. The deep Gulf of Panama, on the Pacific, bends the greater part of the Isthmus into a semicircle.

Instead of running north and south, as you would naturally suppose, the Isthmus runs almost due east and west. That is because South America lies much farther to the east than most of us realize; so much so, that if an airship were to fly far enough in a bee line from New York to the south, it would find itself over the Pacific, off the coast of Peru. At Panama, the Pacific, instead of being west of the Atlantic, is southeast of it. That is why the Spaniards, coming overland to this new ocean from the one they had left on the north, called it the "South Sea." A glance at the map on page 4 will make this plain. It sorely puzzles the visitor to the Isthmus to find the points of the compass apparently so badly twisted, particularly when he sees the sun rise out of the Pacific and set in the Atlantic.

Though the two oceans are so near together at this point, there is a great difference in the rise and fall of their tides. The harbor of the city of Panama, on the Pacific side, where there is twenty feet of water at high tide, is nothing but a mud-flat at low tide, and the townspeople walk out among the stranded boats, and hold a market there (see page 213). The tide comes rushing in, when it rises, in a great wave or bore, something like that in the Bay of Fundy, with a heavy roar that can be heard far inland on a still night. But at Colon, on the Atlantic, the rise and fall of the tide is less than two feet. This curious fact, that the tides rise and fall ten times as far on one side of the Isthmus as on the other, is doubtless what has caused the wide-spread belief that at Panama one ocean is higher than the other. People who say that, forget that the waters of the Atlantic and Pacific meet at Cape Horn, and that sea-level is sea-level the world over.

AREA OF HEATED ROCK IN CULEBRA CUT.
Once thought to be a volcano.

MANGOES.

Panama is about eight hundred miles from the equator, in the same latitude as Mindanao in the Philippines. Its climate is thoroughly tropical. Gilbert, the only poet the Isthmus has ever produced, summed it up neatly in the first stanza of one of his best-known poems, "The Land of the Cocoanut Tree":

> Away down South in the Tropic Zone;
> North latitude nearly nine,
> When the eight month's pour is past and o'er,
> The sun four months doth shine;
> Where it 's eighty-six the year around,
> And people rarely agree;
> Where the plantain grows and the hot wind blows,
> Lies the Land of the Cocoanut Tree.

"Eighty-six the year around" may seem an underestimate but, as a matter of fact, the mercury stays very close to that point from year's end to year's end, seldom rising above ninety. (The temperature of a hundred and twenty, spoken of on page 3, was only found in the deepest parts of the Gaillard Cut at noon.) At night it is always cool enough to necessitate a light covering, and never so hot that one cannot sleep, as it too often is in a Northern summer. It is always summer in Panama, and no hotter in August than in December. Snow-storms and cold weather are, of course, unknown, though three times since the Americans established a weather bureau on the Isthmus it has recorded brief local showers of hail.

Instead of four seasons, there are two: the rainy and the dry. From April to the end of November it rains very frequently, not every clay, as is sometimes declared, but often enough and hard enough to fill, in those nine months, a tank from twelve to fifteen feet deep. With so much rain, and an ocean on either hand, the dampness and humidity are very great. Mold gathers on belts and shoes; guns and razors become rusty unless coated with oil; books must not be left outside air-tight glass cases or they will fall to pieces; and every sunshiny day the clothes closets are emptied and the garments hung out to air.

At that time of year it is easy to realize why houses on the Isthmus are built up in the air on concrete legs; and the morning paper announces that the Chagres River has risen forty feet in two days and is still rising. The rainfall is much heavier on the Atlantic side than the Pacific. They have a saying at Colon that there are two seasons on the Isthmus, the wet and the rainy; and the people of that town used to boast that it rained there every day in the year. But their local pride had a sad fall at the end of the record dry season of 1912. At Colon, as well as elsewhere, it had not rained for months, wide cracks had opened in the hard, dry ground, and the whole country-side was as brown and ragged as an old cigar. When at last "the rains broke" at Ancon, over on the Pacific side, in a magnificent cloudburst—six solid inches of water in three hours—they were still carrying drinking-water to Colon in barges, and had to borrow Ancon's new motor fire-engine to pump it through the mains.

CULEBRA CUT, LOOKING NORTH
When completed, the bottom of the canal will be forty-five feet below the level shown in this picture.

When the rains have come, it is a wonderful sight to see how quickly the old, half-dead vegetation disappears, and the new green stuff comes rushing up. Though the soil is not rich, the heat and moisture cause plants to grow with incredible speed and rankness. Fence-posts sprout and become young trees. The stone-ballasted roadbed of the Panama Railroad has to be sprayed twice a month with crude oil to keep down the weeds. On either side of the track for the greater part of the way across the Isthmus stretches unbroken jungle, rising like a wall at the edge of the cuttings, or lying like a great, green sea below the embankments. It is a thoroughly satisfactory jungle, every bit as good as the pictures in the school geographies. High above the rest tower the tall ceiba trees, great soft woods larger than the largest oak. Besides these and the native cedars, there are mahogany, lignum-vitæ, coco-bolo, and other hardwoods. Some of these are exported for lumber, others the natives hollow out into canoes, some of which are of incredible size. I have seen a dugout, made from one gigantic tree trunk, so large that it was decked over and rigged as a two-masted schooner.

Under the trees, the ground is clogged with dense masses of tangled undergrowth, bound together with thorny creepers, and the rope-like tendrils of the liana vine. Worst of all to travel through are the mangrove swamps near the sea, for the branches of these bushes bend down to the ground and take root, so that it is like trying to walk through a wilderness of croquet wickets. Both here and in the jungle, a path must be cut with the machete, a straight, broad-bladed knife between three and four feet long, that is the great tool and weapon of tropical America. A skilled *machatero*, or wielder of the machete, can cut a trail through the jungle as fast as he cares to walk down it.

MAN O' WARSMAN.

THE FLAT ARCH IN THE RUINS OF SAN DOMINGO
CHURCH, PANAMA CITY

The great tree of Panama is the palm. There are said to be one hundred different species on the Isthmus. Most beautiful of all is the stately royal palm, brought by the French from Cuba to fill the parks and line the avenues. More useful is the native cocoanut palm, that grows everywhere, both in and out of cultivation. Several million cocoanuts are exported from the Isthmus every year. The brown, fuzzy shell of the cocoanut, as we know it in the grocery store at home, is only the innermost husk. As it grows on the tree, the cocoanut is as big as a football, and as smooth and green as an olive. Cut through the thick husk of a green cocoanut with a machete, and you have a pint or more of a thin, milky liquid that is one of the best thirst-quenchers in the world. When the nut is ripe the husk falls off and the milk solidifies into hard, white meat. When this is cut up into small pieces and covered with a little warm water, a thick, rich cream will rise, which cannot be distinguished from the finest cow's cream. Ice cream and custards can be made from this cream, and they will not have the slightest flavor of cocoanut. If, however, this cocoanut cream is churned, it will turn into cocoanut butter, which is good for sunburn, but not for the table. The nuts of the vegetable ivory palm are shipped to the United States to be cut up into imitation ivory collar-buttons.

A native Panamanian will take his machete, cut down and shred a number of palm-branches, and with them thatch the roof of his mud-floored hut, which is built of bamboos bound together with natural cords of liana. Then with the same useful instrument he will scratch the ground and plant a few bananas, plantains—big coarse bananas that are eaten fried—and yams—a sort of sweet potato—and they will take care of themselves until he is ready to harvest the crop. He can burn enough charcoal to cook his dinner, and gather and sell enough cocoanuts to buy the few yards of cloth needed to clothe himself and his family, and spend the rest on hound dogs, fighting-cocks, and lottery tickets. He can grow his own tobacco, and distill his own sugar-cane rum. Now that the Americans have put an end to the revolutions, the poor man on the Isthmus has not a care in the world, and is probably the laziest and happiest person on earth.

Besides bananas—which, by the way, grow the other way up from the way they hang by the door of the grocery—many different kinds of fruit are found in Panama. Mangoes and alligator-pears are great favorites with American visitors. On the Island of Taboga, in the Bay of Panama, grow some of the best pineapples in the world; not the little woody things we know in the North, but luscious big lumps of sugary pulp, soft enough to eat with a spoon. You have never tasted a pineapple until you have eaten a "Taboga pine."

Flowers are as abundant as fruit. There are whole trees full of gorgeous blossoms at certain seasons. Roses bloom during the greater part of the year and rare and valuable orchids abound in the jungle. If the Republic of Panama ever adopts a national flower, it should be that strange and beautiful orchid found only on the Isthmus, that the Spaniards called "El Espiritu Santo," the flower of the Holy Ghost. When it blooms, which it does only every other year, the petals fold back, revealing the perfectly formed figure of a tiny dove.

THE "HOLY GHOST ORCHID."

It is true that the flowers on the Isthmus have no perfume, but it does not follow, as is so frequently declared, that the birds of Panama have no song. I have often heard them in the mating season, at the beginning of the rains, chirping and twittering as gaily as any birds in the Northern woods. Most conspicuous of all, among the feathered folk of the Isthmus, are the great black buzzards and "men-o' warsmen," so named because they wheel about over the city in large flocks, manœuvering with the precision of a squadron of battleships. Formerly, these birds were the only scavengers, all refuse being thrown out into the street for them to eat. They will soar and circle for many minutes with hardly a beat of their broad wings. When the first aeroplane (a small Moissant monoplane), came to Panama and flew among a flock of buzzards, it was difficult for a man on the ground to tell the machine from the birds. Other large fliers are the pelicans, while tall, dignified blue herons and white cranes walk mincingly through the swamps. Parrots of all sizes abound, from big gaudy macaws, with beaks like tinsmiths' shears, to dainty little green parrakeets, that the engineers call "working-models of parrots." Tiniest and loveliest of all are the bright-colored humming-birds.

There are not many large mammals native to the Isthmus, and most of these have been hunted until they are now hard to find. The last time that a "lion," as the natives call the jaguar—a black or dark-brown member of the cat tribe, as big as a St. Bernard dog—was seen in the city of Panama, it was brought there in a cage and advertised to appear in a ferocious "bull and lion fight," at the bull-ring. When the cage door was opened in the ring, the jaguar jumped over the tenfoot barricade into the audience, bounded up the nearest aisle to the top of the grandstand, leaped down, and was last seen heading for the jungle. No one was hurt, for everybody gave him plenty of room. Another much-advertised beast that is seldom seen is the tapir, a fat black grass-eater, that looks like a miniature elephant with a very short trunk. Deer are still fairly abundant, pretty little things, not much bigger than a North American jack-rabbit. Centuries ago there were large numbers of warrees, or wild hogs, and of long-tailed, black-and-white monkeys, "the ugliest I ever saw," wrote Captain Dampier, the bucaneer naturalist. But to shoot either of these today, a hunter would have to go deep into the jungle. Perhaps the most curious-looking animal on the Isthmus is the armadillo, "the little armored one," the Spaniards called him, because of the heavy rings of natural plate-mail that protect him against the teeth and claws of his enemies, as do the quills of the Northern porcupine.

ARMADILLO.

Reptiles are well represented on the Isthmus, though snakes are very much scarcer in the Canal Zone than one would naturally suppose. Only a few small boa-constrictors—eight feet long or so—were killed during the building of the Canal, and there is no case of a laborer having been fatally bitten by a poisonous snake, although both the coral-snake and the *fer-de-lance* are said to be found in Panama. Old stone ruins, that in the North would be swarming with blacksnakes and adders, seem here to be entirely given over to the lizards. Lizards are everywhere, and of all sizes, from three inches long to five or six feet. These big fellows are called iguanas, and look remarkably like dragons out of a fairy-book, except that they have no wings and do not breathe fire and smoke. They are quite harmless, and eagerly hunted by the natives, because their flesh, when well stewed, tastes like chicken. One of the old chroniclers speaks of these lizards as "'guanas, which make good broth."

IGUANA.

CROCODILE.

Far more formidable than the harmless lizards are the great man-eating crocodiles that swarm in the rivers of Panama. They are not alligators, as is usually and incorrectly stated, for the alligator is a smaller, broader-muzzled beast, that does not attack men. The American crocodile, usually confused with the alligator, is larger and much more ferocious, and has a longer and sharper head. Many a man who has been upset in a canoe on the Chagres, or who has walked too near what looked like a rotting log stranded on the bank, has been caught and eaten by a crocodile. Parties of Americans are often organized to hunt and kill these dangerous reptiles.

BRIDGE AT THE ENTRANCE TO OLD PANAMA
Over three hundred years old.

Man-eating sharks are found in the waters on either side of the Isthmus, as well as an abundance of Spanish mackerel, and other food fish. Indeed, the name "Panama" means, in the old Indian tongue, "a place abounding in fish." There is not much chance that the different breeds of the two oceans will have a chance to mingle by swimming through the canal, unless they are able to swim uphill through locks and sluices, and through a fresh-water lake.

Though men and other animals are sluggish and lazy in the tropics, it is there that insects show the greatest vitality and activity. The big black ants go marching about at night in small armies, and negroes are hired to follow them till they find their nests, which they then pour full of an explosive liquid and blow up. Well-defined ant trails, an inch or so wide, run through the jungle, and even at noon they are crowded with hurrying passengers, every fourth or fifth ant carrying a bit of green leaf by way of a parasol. A corner of a cinder tennis court that was built for the officers of the battalion of marines at Camp Elliott blocked one of these ant paths, and the ants kept cutting it down to the former level, no matter how often the soldiers filled it up. Little red ants swarm in all the houses, however well they are kept. Sugar, candy, and all other sweet things are only safe on top of inverted tumblers standing in bowls of water, for nothing short of a moat will keep out the ants. But at the same time, this stagnant water may be serving as a breeding-place for mosquitoes. There used to be over forty different kinds of mosquitos on the Isthmus, but nowadays they are very rare.

Another insect pest, however, that has not been abated is the famous "red bug," a tiny tick, smaller than the head of a pin, but big enough to make plenty of trouble. The red bugs live in the grass, and burrow under the skin of human beings and animals and breed there until they are dug out with the point of a knife. Other species of ticks attack horses, cattle and fowls, and are a great pest to farmers in that country. Compared to them the more picturesque and widely feared scorpions and tarantulas do almost no harm. Both the scorpion, who looks like a small lobster with his tail bent up over his head and a sting at the end of it, and the tarantula, a huge spider covered with stiff black hair, are hideously ugly, and their bite or sting is intensely painful. But it is not fatal, as is commonly and erroneously supposed, and for every man that is hurt by a scorpion or tarantula, hundreds of dollars' worth of damage is done by ticks and red bugs.

Before the white men came, there was a large native population on the Isthmus. Some of the Spanish chroniclers place the number of Indians as high as two millions; almost certainly there were more of them than the three hundred and fifty thousand persons, of all races (see page 244), that inhabit that country today. The life of the early Indian was not unlike that of the poorer Panamanian of the present. He wore less clothing and his women made it of cocoanut fiber instead of imported cotton cloth; instead of a steel machete he used a sort of hardwood sword called a *macana*, and he hunted and fought with bow and spear instead of firearms. But the *bohio* or thatched hut, the *cayuca* or dug-out canoe, the rude farming and the fishing, have scarcely changed at all.

The Isthmian Indians are very skilful boatmen and fishermen. Their canoes are often seen in Colon harbor, where they come to sell their catch. These Indians belong to the Tule or San Blas tribe, that occupy and rule the Atlantic side of the Isthmus, from about forty miles east of Colon to South America.

SAN BLAS INDIANS IN VARIOUS COSTUMES.

The Pacific side of this part of Panama is held by another tribe of Indians, the Chucunaques. Both pride themselves on keeping their race pure, despise the mongrel, half-breed Panamanians, and forbid white men to settle in their country. People who complain that the San Blas and the Chucunaques are "treacherous," and "inhospitable" forget that they are the survivors of a race once hunted down by the white men with fire and sword and bloodhounds for their gold. In appearance, the San Blas are short, stocky, little fellows, many of them looking remarkably like Japanese.

SAN BLAS INDIAN SQUAWS.
Sitting with American canal employees on a dug-out
canoe in a San Blas coast town.
White men are not allowed ashore after sundown.

The narrowest part of the Isthmus is in the San Blas country, and has long been a favorite among the many proposed routes for an interoceanic canal. To give anything like a complete list of the various canal routes would be to review most of the history of the discovery and exploration of America. From the Straits of Magellan to Hudson's Bay, the early navigators sought for an open passage between the two oceans. Later, whenever explorers or engineers found a place where the continent was narrow, or broken by large rivers, or lakes, proposals were made for an artificial waterway. From the middle of the sixteenth century to the end of the nineteenth, the routes most favored were the five marked by letters on the map of *Five canal routes*.

PART OF THE CHARGES RIVER.

Now in the bed of Gatun Lake, with its banks cut down to make a five hundred foot channel.

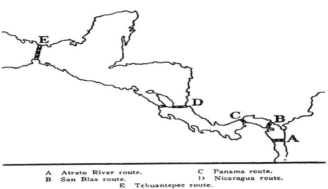

A Atrato River route.   C Panama route.
B San Blas route.   D Nicaragua route.
              E Tehuantepec route.

A Atrato River route.
B San Blas route.
C Panama route.
D Nicaragua route.
E Tehuantepec route.

MAP OF FIVE CANAL ROUTES.

30

A- The Darien or Atrato River route. The distance between the headwaters of the Darien River, flowing into the Gulf of Uraba, and the source of the nearest small river running into the Pacific, is very short. Canoes could be easily carried from one stream to another. There is a story that a village priest, at the end of the eighteenth century, had his parishioners dig a ditch, so that loaded canoes could be floated across the divide, without a portage. Whether or not that is so, it would be impossible for even the smallest modern cargo-boat to steam up a mountain creek, through such a ditch, and down the rock-strewn rapids of the upper Atrato. The divide is too high and the supply of water too scanty at this point for the construction of a ship canal suited for twentieth-century commerce.

B- The San Blas route. Here, where the distance from sea to sea is only about thirty miles, Balboa crossed to the Pacific in 1513. Shortly afterwards, this country was abandoned to the Indians, except for a brief time in 1788, when an attempt was made to establish a line of posts, and a Spanish officer succeeded in crossing to the Pacific, but was not allowed to return. Interest in this region was revived by the lying reports of two adventurers, Cullen and Gisborne, who declared that they had easily crossed and recrossed the San Blas country, and found the summit-level of the divide only a hundred and fifty feet high. Induced by these falsehoods (Cullen had never been to the Isthmus, and Gisborne not more than six miles inland), a small expedition under Lieutenant Strain, U.S.N., started from Caledonia Bay, on the Atlantic side, to march to the Gulf of San Miguel on the Pacific, in January, 1854. After suffering fearful hardships and losing one-third of their number from starvation, Lieutenant Strain and the others succeeded in reaching their goal. They were followed, in 1870-1, by several strong and well-equipped naval expeditions, whose surveys proved that the summit-level is at least a thousand feet above the sea. It was then proposed to build a canal there by boring a great tunnel through the mountains; but the rapidly increasing size of ships has made this out of the question.

C- The Panama or Chagres River route. There is no truth in the story that Columbus sailed up the Chagres River and so came within twelve miles of the Pacific; but the Spaniards soon found out that the easiest way across the Isthmus was to pole or paddle up this river, and then go by road to the Pacific. The first proposal for digging a Panama canal: a shallow ditch between the head of navigation on the Chagres and the South Sea, was made as early as 1529. The Emperor Charles V not only opposed this project, but even forbade its being brought forward again, under penalty of death; ostensibly because of the impiety of the idea of joining two oceans that God had put asunder, but, really, because such a canal would give the enemies of Spain too easy access to her Pacific colonies. The later history of the Chagres route occupies the greater part of this book.

D- The Nicaragua route. The broad surface of Lake Nicaragua, and the San Juan River, that flows out of it into the Atlantic, make this seem a most obvious place for an interoceanic canal. Though much dredging of channels and building of breakwaters would be needed to make a safe harbor at either end, and expensive locks and dams would have to be built before large steamers could navigate the river and the lake, the same disadvantages had to be overcome at Panama. The greater length of a canal at Nicaragua,—the continent at this point is one hundred and fifty miles wide,—and the closer proximity of more or less active volcanoes, with the greater danger of eruptional earthquakes, would make it inferior to the canal at Panama. The continual revolutions and political disturbances of Nicaragua, which has been so badly governed that no foreign government or private company has been willing to risk the investment of the hundreds of million of dollars needed to build a canal there, finally turned the scale against that country. Nicaragua is probably the only other place, beside Panama, where it would be physically possible to build a modern ship canal across the American continent.

E. The Tehuantepec route. Not long after the Spaniards, under Cortez, had conquered Mexico, they built a road across the Isthmus of Tehuantepec, which is the narrowest part of that country. Centuries ago, there was more than a little trade by this road, between Spain and Mexico and the Far

East, as was proved by the discovery at Vera Cruz of two large bronze cannon bearing the stamp of the old Manila foundry. The Isthmus of Tehuantepec is too wide and the summit-level too high, to be pierced by a sea-level canal; and the supply of water is too scanty for a canal with locks. When the French were trying to dig a canal at Panama, an American engineer, Captain Eads, proposed to build across Tehuantepec a "ship-railway": a railroad with a very broad gage, on which huge flat-cars would carry the largest vessels of the time from ocean to ocean. Like the Darien ship-tunnel, the increasing size of ships made this ingenious project impossible. The present Tehuantepec Railroad is a standard gage road, doing a thriving business in carrying transcontinental freight. This has been temporarily, if not permanently, reduced by the opening of the Panama Canal.

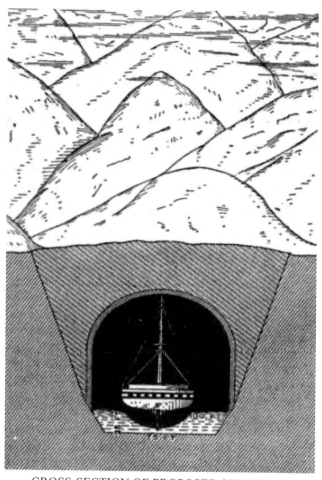

CROSS-SECTION OF PROPOSED SHIP TUNNEL,
SAN BLAS ROUTE.

CHAPTER II
HOW COLUMBUS SOUGHT FOR THE STRAIT

If you go to Panama by ship from one of our Atlantic ports, the first land you will see is Watling's Island, or San Salvador, where Columbus caught his first glimpse of the New World in 1492. We know that this is one of the Bahamas, but Columbus died in the belief that it was an island off the coast of Asia. For though he rightly supposed the world to be round so that by sailing long enough to the west you could reach the east, neither he nor any one else in Europe at the time realized how long a voyage that would be. And the last thing Columbus imagined was that he should find a whole New World.

According to his calculations, Japan must lie just about where he found Cuba, and so Columbus told his crew, and made them all take oath that Cuba *was* Japan. Now, he reasoned, it could be only a little distance further to the rich cities and kingdoms of the Far East. Wonderful stories of their wealth and luxury had been brought back to Europe by Marco Polo, the Venetian, and other travelers, who had made the long difficult journey overland from Europe to India, or even China. And for countless centuries the silks and spices, the gold and jewels, of the East had been carried to the West over caravan-trails that were trodden deep before the first Pharaoh ruled in Egypt. Do you know why they have the same fairy stories and folk-lore in Ireland that they have in Japan? Because they passed from lip to lip, from camp-fire to camp-fire along this old trade-route, no one knows how many thousand years ago.

STATUE OF COLUMBUS AT MADRID.

But in the fifteenth century the Turks captured Constantinople and closed the overland road. This threw the whole world out of gear. The Portuguese were the first to look for a new way to India, by sailing round Africa. And in 1487, the brave captain, Bartholomew Diaz, succeeded in rounding the "Cape of Storms," and came back with the news that he had entered the Indian Ocean, and that there was good hope of reaching India by that route. So the King of Portugal commanded the "Cape of Storms" to be rechristened the "Cape of Good Hope," and so it is called to this day.

Bartholomew Columbus was on this voyage and talked it over with his brother Christopher, who pointed out how much easier and shorter it would be to sail twenty-five hundred or perhaps three thousand miles straight across the Atlantic to Asia, than to make the long trip of more than twelve thousand miles round Africa. The idea was not new, but the king of Portugal would have none of it; and you know what a bitter, weary time Columbus had at the court of Spain. All these black memories must have seemed to fade like small clouds far astern, as he sailed back to Palos with the glad news that he had discovered the outposts of Asia, and that another voyage or two would surely open the direct passage to the East Indies. But more than four hundred and twenty years were to pass before that passage was to be opened.

Columbus discovered more islands on his second voyage, and on the third came to the mainland of South America, at the mouth of the Orinoco. So great a body of fresh water as here poured into the ocean could flow from no mere island but from a continent, "a Terra Firma, of vast extent, of which until this day nothing has been known."

This made one mainland, or "firm land," as the Spaniards called it, from some idea that a continent must be made of solider stuff than an island; and north of it, Cuba must make another. For at this time no one had sailed round, and this island Cuba or "Japan" was supposed to be part of the mainland of Asia. Somewhere between these two bodies of land, thought Columbus, must be a strait through which flowed the waters of the Atlantic into the Indian Ocean, causing the strong current to the west that was felt as far north as Santo Domingo. Once through the strait, instead of tamely retracing his course, he would sail round the world, and home to Spain by way of the Cape of Good Hope. By this he hoped to eclipse the success of Vasco de Gama, who had at last realized the "good hope" of reaching India by way of the Cape, and returned to Portugal, laden with glory and riches in 1499.

CHORRERA, A TYPICAL TOWN IN THE INTERIOR
OF THE REPUBLIC OF PANAMA.

It was now 1502, ten years after the discovery of America, when Columbus sailed on his fourth and last voyage. He had four ships, the *Capitana*, *Santiago de Palos*, *Gallego*, and *Biscaina*. The largest of these was but of seventy tons burden, the smallest of fifty, and all were worn and old. The crews numbered a hundred and fifty men and boys, there were provisions for two years, and both cannon and trinkets for winning gold from the Indians. Bartholomew Columbus was captain of one of the caravels, with the title of Adelantado, and with his father on the flagship was Christopher Columbus's thirteen-year-old son, Ferdinand. When he grew up, Ferdinand Columbus wrote a biography of his father, containing the best account we have of this voyage.

They sailed from Cadiz on the ninth of May, 1502, took on wood and water at the Canaries, and put in at Santo Domingo, to exchange one of the ships for another, "because it was a bad sailer, and, besides, could carry no sail, but the side would lie almost under water." But Ovando, the governor of the Spanish colony there, was an enemy of Columbus, and refused to let him have a new ship, or even to take refuge in the harbor from a threatening storm. Ovando himself was just setting forth for Spain, in a great fleet of his own, laden with much gold that had been cruelly wrung from the poor Indians, including one nugget so large that the Spaniards had used it for a table. Columbus warned Ovando that a storm was coming, and was laughed at for his pains. But scarcely had the governor's fleet set sail, when down upon it swooped a terrible West Indian hurricane, and sent most of the ships to the bottom, big nugget and all. One ship, the poorest of the fleet, reached Spain, with some of Columbus's own goods on board. On one of the few vessels that struggled back to Santo Domingo was Rodrigo de Bastidas, of whom we shall hear more presently.

Columbus's own little squadron weathered the storm, thanks to the admiral's seamanship, which to the Spanish sailors appeared "art magic." Steering once more in the direction of the supposed strait, they were carried by the currents to the south of Cuba. There they fell in near the Isle of Pines, with a great canoe "of eight feet beam, and as long as a Spanish galley." Its owner, a *cacique* of Yucatan, was on a trading voyage, with a cargo of copper hatchets and cups, cloaks and tunics of dyed cotton, daggers and wooden swords edged with obsidian glass, and, strangest of all to the eyes of the Spaniards, a supply of *cacao* (chocolate) beans. Here was evidence of something far superior to the naked savagery of the islands. It began to look as if Columbus would have some use for the Arabic interpreters he had brought with him, together with letters to the Great Khan of Tartary.

CARAVEL.

And indeed, if the old Indian that the admiral took on board for a guide had piloted the Spaniards to his own country, they would have found there great cities and stone temples and hoards of gold to their hearts' content. But when they had come to

Cape Honduras, where the shore of Central America runs east and west, they asked the old Indian which way the gold came from. He pointed to the east, away from his own country, and so Yucatan and Mexico were left to be conquered by Cortez in 1517.

Fighting against head winds—once they made but sixty leagues in seventy days—the little fleet struggled on down the coast. The first Indians they met with had such large holes bored in their ears that the Spaniards called that region "the Coast of the Ear." Better weather came after rounding Cape Gracias à Dios, or "Thanks to God," and the Indians offered to trade with *guanin*, a mixture of gold and copper. Pure gold, they said, was to be found further down the coast. So Columbus kept on, past what are now Nicaragua and Costa Rica, until he came to the great Chiriqui Lagoon. Here were plenty of gold ornaments, in the form of eagles, frogs, or other creatures, such as are dug up today from the ancient Indian graves in the Province of Chiriqui. Among them we often find little bells of pure gold, shaped exactly like our sleigh bells, but Columbus does not mention them. Ferdinand Columbus does speak of finding something a little further down the coast that seems even stranger: the ruins of a stone wall, a piece of which they brought away "as a memorial of that antiquity."

The strait was now reported to be near at hand, so the interpreters declared; just beyond a country called Veragua, rich in gold. Eagerly they sped on, passing Veragua with a fair wind that carried them by Limon Bay, where we are now digging the Atlantic entrance of the strait they sought.

The admiral put in at a land-locked, natural harbor, so beautiful that he called it Porto Bello, by which name it has been known ever since. After a week's rest here he pushed on to a number of islands full of wild corn, which he called the Port of Provisions. Finally, on the twenty-fourth of November, he made his furthest harbor, a forgotten little cove named El Retrete, or the Closet.

Here the search for the strait ended. Another white man had been over the ground beyond this, Bastidas, who had escaped from the hurricane at Santo Domingo, and almost certainly met Columbus there. From the Orinoco to Cape Honduras no break had been found in the barrier between the two oceans. So they turned back, battered by storms and terrified by a great waterspout, which, says Ferdinand Columbus, they dissolved by reciting the Gospel of St. John. In Veragua they tried gold-hunting, and attempted to found a colony, but the Indians, under a crafty *cacique*, rose against them. After hard fighting, and an Odyssey of misfortunes, the Spaniards were forced to flee. They left the hulk of the *Gallego*, behind them and the *Biscaina* at Porto Bello. The two remaining caravels, bored through and through by the teredo worm, staggered as far as the coast of Jamaica, to be beached there, side by side. Two rotting wrecks, and the barren title of "Duke of Veragua," by which his descendants are known to this day, were all that Christopher Columbus brought back from the Isthmus of Panama.

RUINS AT PORTO BELLO
Probably old Spanish custom house

CHAPTER III
HOW THE SPANIARDS SETTLED IN DARIEN

Columbus having reported that there was gold in Veragna, the King of Spain decided to found a colony there, and another beyond the Gulf of Uraba, where Bastidas had found pearls and gold. Into this gulf flowed a river so great that it filled the bay with fresh water at low tide. This river, which is now called the Atrato, was then called the Darien, and it has given that name to all the South American end of the Isthmus.

Christopher Columbus died, a broken-hearted old man, in 1506, but his brother Bartholomew, the Adelantado, was alive and anxious to colonize the "Dukedom" of Veragua. But Queen Isabella, their patron, was also dead, and the greedy King Ferdinand was jealous of their family, and wanted these new gold-fields for the crown. So he appointed a court favorite, Diego de Nicuesa, to be governor of all the land between Cape Gracias à Dios, and the Gulf of Uraba. This was made the province of Castilla del Oro, or Golden Castille.

The poorer land east and south of the gulf was called Nueva Andalucia (New Andalusia) and given to Alonso de Ojeda, a bold explorer, the first to have followed Columbus to the New World. On that voyage, in 1499, Ojeda had had with him the Florentine merchant's clerk, Americus Vespucius, who has given his name to the whole New World.

Both the new governors were small men, well built and in the prime of life. Ojeda was a famous athlete, who had once, by way of showing his prowess before the Queen, gone out on a narrow piece of timber that projected twenty feet from the top of the Giralda tower at Seville, "walked along it as fast as if it had been a brick floor, and at the end of the plank lifted one foot in the air, turned, and walked back as quickly. Then he went to the bottom of the tower, placed one foot against the wall, and threw an orange to the top, a height of two hundred and fifty feet." He was a rough, reckless, bull-headed fighter. Nicuesa, on the contrary, was of noble descent and polished manners, a skilled musician and orator, and a great favorite at court. Both alike were lacking in the thing most essential in a leader, the power of managing men.

Both expeditions sailed from Santo Domingo. Ojeda got away first, on the tenth of November, 1509, with two ships, two brigantines, three hundred men and twelve mares. Nicuesa, the wealthier of the two, had spent all his money and more in equipping a larger fleet, and just as he was getting into his boat, he was arrested for debt. After ten days' delay a friend advanced the money, and Nicuesa set sail with two large ships, a caravel, and two brigantines, carrying a force of six hundred and fifty men.

AMERICUS VESPUCIUS.

Born at Florence, Italy, in 1452; entered commercial
service in Spain; accompanied four expeditions to the New
World, on the first of which, in 1497, he claimed to have
reached the continent of America before the Cabots and
Columbus; died at Seville in 1512.

Ojeda, in the meanwhile, had reached the harbor
where the present city of Cartagena was founded in
1531. In spite of the warning of his second in
command, old Juan de la Cosa, that the Indians
hereabouts were hard fighters and used poisoned
arrows, Ojeda landed with seventy men, and
attacked one of their towns. The Indians fled, Ojeda
allowed his men to scatter in pursuit, and the

Indians, suddenly rallying, killed with their darts and poisoned arrows, every Spaniard of the party but Ojeda and one follower. Ojeda's great strength enabled him to break through, and his small size made it possible for him to hide well behind his shield. Indeed, when his other men found him, half dead with exhaustion but unwounded, there were the marks of three hundred arrows on it.

Nicuesa's fleet came sailing by, and he gladly lent his aid, particularly to avenge the death of Juan de la Cosa, who was one of the ambushed party and had been an old and beloved pilot of Columbus. The two governors fell on the Indians at night with four hundred men, and slaughtered a great number. Then Nicuesa sailed away to Veragua, and Ojeda entered the Gulf of Uraba and founded a town on his side of it, calling it San Sebastian.

But here there were only more poisoned arrows, and neither gold nor provisions. A ship load of food bought from a gang of pirates who had stolen it, kept the colony alive for a while. When this was gone, Ojeda sailed on the pirate craft to bring help from Santo Domingo. He left San Sebastian in charge of his lieutenant, Francisco Pizarro, of whom history had a great deal more to say. If Ojeda did not return at the end of fifty days, they were to take the two brigantines and go where they pleased.

When the fifty days were up, Ojeda and such of the pirates as were yet alive were struggling along, up to their armpits in mud, through mangrove swamps on the coast of Cuba, where they had been shipwrecked. When at last they were rescued by the

Governor of Jamaica and brought to Santo Domingo (where the pirates were all hanged), Ojeda was a ruined and worn-out man. Like many another fighter of that brave, cruel age, he became a monk shortly before his death, "making," in the words of the historian Oviedo, "a more praiseworthy end than other captains in these parts have done."

Pizarro and his men waited the fifty days and a little longer, for the two brigantines would not hold them all. After enough had died of starvation and arrow-poison to make room for the rest, they sailed to Carthagena, losing one brigantine by the way. In the harbor they found reinforcements from Santo Domingo, commanded by a lawyer named Enciso, who held office under Governor Ojeda. He had with him one hundred and fifty men, with horses, arms, powder and provisions. But the most important part of his cargo was a barrel with a man in it.

This man was Vasco Nuñez de Balboa, who had made a failure of farming on Santo Domingo, and since debtors were not allowed to leave the island, had had a friend smuggle him aboard in this fashion. When the cask had been opened, early in the voyage, the indignant Enciso was for setting him ashore on a desert island, but was persuaded not to do so. Now the pedantic lawyer turned on Pizarro's starving wretches, accused them of desertion, and insisted on their going back with him to San Sebastian. On the way, they were all shipwrecked again, and when they arrived at their destination they found the fort and settlement utterly destroyed, the Indians fiercer than ever, and no food. What was to be done?

Balboa showed the way. He had sailed this way before, with Bastidas, and across the gulf they had found both food and gold, on the shores of the river Darien. Most important of all, the Indians there used no poisoned arrows.

At once Enciso and Balboa, with a hundred men-at-arms, crossed to the western shore, where five hundred warriors were drawn up to meet them. Kneeling devoutly on the beach, the Spaniards vowed that if victorious they would dedicate both the spoils and their first settlement to the shrine, much reverenced in Seville, of Santa Maria de la Antigua. Then, rising, they rushed like starving wolves on the Indians. There was no poison in their arrows, and those that were not cut down in the first charge fled at once.

Provisions and gold were found in the Indian town, San Sebastian was abandoned, and Enciso founded the town of Santa Maria de la Antigua de Darien. But it was another thing to rule the rough men that lived there. They had had enough of Enciso's ways, which were better suited for a law court than a frontier, and Balboa showed them how to get rid of him. They were now on the western side of the gulf, in Nicuesa's territory, and no one claiming authority under Ojeda had any power there. Balboa was a real leader of men, Enciso was not. The lawyer was deposed and Nicuesa invited to come and rule them.

OLD SPANISH PORT AT PORTO BELLO

"NOMBRE DE DIOS"—STREET SCENE.

But what had become of Nicuesa? His fleet had been wrecked on the shore of Veragua, and he and the other survivors had struggled down the coast, sometimes afloat, sometimes wading through the swamps, always suffering incredible hardships. At last they came to Porto Bello, where one who had sailed with the "old admiral," as the Spaniards of that time called Columbus, recognized the anchor of the *Biscaina*. But the Indians killed twenty of them, and the rest fled to another port further east. "In God's name" (or, in Spanish, *en nombre de Dios*), cried the first man who stepped ashore, "let us stay here." And for that reason "Nombre de Dios" has been the name of that port ever since.

Of the six hundred and fifty men who had left Santo Domingo with Nicuesa, only a hundred reached Nombre de Dios, thirty of these soon died, the rest were so weak with hunger they could scarcely lift their weapons, and there was not one left strong enough to act as sentinel. Imagine their joy when a caravel came from the east, bringing Nicuesa's lieutenant, Colmenares, with supplies. He found the once handsome and elegant Nicuesa "of all living men the most unfortunate, in a manner dried up with extreme hunger, filthy and horrible to behold"; informed him of the new settlement at Antigua, and that he had been elected its governor.

This sudden change of fortune was too much for the poor little courtier. Instead of showing any gratitude, he declared that these men of Ojeda's had no right to settle in his country and that he would take away all the gold they had collected there. This news got to Antigua before him, and he was met at the beach by an armed mob. Balboa tried his best to save him, but in vain. They thrust the unfortunate Nicuesa and the seventeen men still faithful to him into a wretched, leaky brigantine, and turned him adrift to perish. And perish he did, though whether by land or sea no man can say.

So both the royal governors were gone, and Balboa the stowaway ruled in Darien.

CHAPTER IV
HOW NUNEZ DE BALBOA FOUND THE SOUTH SEA

The first thing Balboa did, after Nicuesa had been thrust forth to die, on March first, 1511, was to get rid both of Enciso and the leaders of the mob. He did this by sending the lawyer back to Spain, and then advising the others to follow and see that he did them no harm at court. He knew perfectly well that Enciso would complain to the King, and that the only excuses acceptable would be plenty of gold. As long as they sent him his royal share of *that*, his majesty cared but little what his loyal subjects did to each other in the far-off Indies. So Balboa looked for gold.

Luck favored him. As the rear-guard of Nicuesa's men were being brought from Nombre de Dios to Antigua they were met by two men, naked and painted like Indians, who addressed them in Spanish. They were sailors who had run away from one of Nicuesa's ships, a year and a half before, and had been kindly received by Careta, an Indian chief. One of them, Juan Alonso, had been made Careta's chief captain, and he basely offered to deliver to them with his own hands Careta, bound, and to betray his master's town to the Spaniards.

Balboa accepted the traitor's offer, marched to the town, and was hospitably received by Careta. After a pretended departure, he returned, rushed the town at night, devastated it, arid carried off Careta and his family to Antigua. This was the ordinary way for Christians to repay Indian hospitality, both then and for a very long time afterwards. But what follows shows that Balboa was both kinder and shrewder than the average Spanish conqueror, who would undoubtedly have put Careta to death, now that he had seized his gold. Balboa, on the contrary, made peace with the chief and married his daughter. They agreed that Careta's people should supply Antigua with food, and the Spaniards help them against their enemies.

So, by matching tribe against tribe, Balboa conquered a great part of Darien. Comogre, the richest chief of all, received him peacefully, with a great present of gold. The Spaniards were weighing this out and squabbling over the division, when the chief's eldest son contemptuously threw the scales to the ground. If they cared for that sort of stuff, he exclaimed, they would find plenty of it to the south. There by a great sea on which they sailed in ships almost as large as those of the Spaniards were a people, who ate and drank out of vessels of gold. Thus the Spaniards heard for the first time of the Pacific and Peru.

Comogre's son offered to guide the white men to this sea and to let them hang him if they did not find it. But Balboa had heard of a wonderful golden temple of Dabaiba, somewhere up the Atrato River, and went up there to find it. He got no further than a country where the Indians lived in the tops of big trees, and dropped things on visitors. Having conquered this tribe, by cutting down the trees, and suppressed an attempted revolt of five chiefs, Balboa loaded a ship with all the gold he could get, and sent it to Spain, to win him favor with the King. Then, as he knew that Enciso and his other enemies at court would be very busy, he decided to overwhelm them with the great news of his discovery of a new ocean.

ENTRANCE TO OLD SPANISH PORT AT PORTO BELLO.

So on the sixth of September, 1513, he set out to cross the Isthmus. Comogre's son had warned him that a thousand men would be needed to fight their way through, but Balboa had faith in his hundred and ninety well-armed Spaniards. They had with them bloodhounds, even more dreaded than themselves by the Indians, a train of native porters, and guides that led them by the best and shortest way. After some easy fighting and hard marching, they reached a hill, from the top of which, the Indians said, "the other ocean" could be seen. Halting his men, Balboa ascended alone, and was the first European to see the Pacific. This was September twenty-third, and it was six days later, on St. Michael's Day, when they reached the nearest part of the Pacific, which is still called, for that reason, the Gulf of San Miguel.

Wading into the great unknown ocean, Balboa took eternal possession, in the name of the King of Spain, of all its waters, and every shore they touched. Today, Spain does not own an inch of land on that ocean. No one can point out the hill from which Balboa first saw the Pacific, and the Isthmus of Darien is less known to white men than it was four hundred years ago.

After a few of the local chiefs had been beaten in battle, and one, a wicked tyrant named Pacra, had been torn to pieces by the Spanish dogs, the others hastened to make friends with Balboa. They brought him a great deal of gold, besides pearls from the islands in the Gulf of San Miguel, and promised to collect much more. Suffering slightly from a fever, but without having lost one of his men, Balboa returned in triumph to Antigua, after an absence of a little less than four months. But it would have been far better for him if his great exploit had been accomplished only a few weeks sooner, so that his messenger could have reached

Spain before the new governor had sailed for Darien. For this new governor who was to succeed Balboa, was the man who is seldom spoken of by his full name, Don Pedro Arias de Avila, but usually by his fearful nickname of "Pedrarias the Cruel."

BALBOA.

CHAPTER V
HOW PEDRARIAS THE CRUEL BUILT OLD PANAMA

Enciso's complaints had decided the king to appoint a new governor, who should call Balboa to account. As usual, he picked a court favorite, Pedro Arias de Avila, called for short, Pedrarias Davila. He had served bravely as a colonel of infantry, and as he was now seventy years old, the king thought he could be counted on to attend strictly to the royal business, without having time to become dangerously powerful. But Pedrarias lived long enough to do more evil than any other man who ever came to the New World, before or since.

The news of Balboa's first successes brought in recruits, who were particularly attracted by the tale of a river so full of gold that the Indians strained it out with nets. Fully fifteen hundred crowded into the ships, instead of the twelve hundred sought for. Light wooden shields and quilted cotton jackets took the place of the steel armor that must have killed more men with sunstroke than it saved from the Indians' arrows. A Spanish historian of the time calls this expedition "the best equipped company that ever left Spain."

When the fleet reached Darien, the silk-clad messengers, sent on shore to seek Balboa, found him sitting in his underclothes and slippers, overseeing some Indians who were thatching a house. Even greater was the contrast when the new governor entered the town next day, with his wife, Dona Isabel, on one hand, and on the other a bishop in robes and miter, with friars chanting the Te Deum, and a train of gaily dressed cavaliers smiling scornfully at the tattered, sunburned colonists.

But not many weeks later, one of these same men in lace and satin staggered through the streets of Antigua, begging in vain for a morsel of food, and finally dropped dead in the sight of all. There was not enough food for such a multitude, and besides, the newcomers died by hundreds of the fevers. This is probably why Pedrarias did not at once put Balboa to death, under the pretext of what he had done to Nicuesa and Enciso. For although he was bitterly jealous of Balboa's success, Pedrarias realized that the other's men were seasoned veterans, and his own were sickly recruits. Besides, the bishop and some of the other officials befriended Balboa. So he was merely fined, imprisoned a few days, and then released. If he had been a wiser man, Balboa would have returned to Spain, where he was now a great hero, but instead, he stayed to watch Pedrarias at his work.

And dreadful work it was. Balboa had killed like a soldier, but Pedrarias tortured like a fiend. He had been instructed to establish a line of posts between the two oceans, and sent his lieutenant, Juan de Ayora, to locate the first fort at a place on the Atlantic coast called Santa Cruz. A chief who spread a feast for him, thinking to welcome his old friend Balboa, was tortured until he gave up all his gold, and then burned alive because it was not enough. As for the other chiefs Ayora caught, "some he roasted alive, some were thrown living to the dogs, some were hanged, and for others were devised new forms of torture." After several months of this, Ayora sneaked back to Antigua, stole a ship, and sailed away with all the gold so infernally won.

Another force crossed to the Pacific side and ravaged there, but were glad to fight their way back again, as all the tribes were rising. They were met by Indians waving the bloody shirts of the garrison of Santa Cruz. The blockhouse there had been stormed, and molten gold poured down the Spaniards' throats, while the Indians cried, "Eat the gold, Christians! Take your fill of gold!"

A hundred and eighty Spaniards, with three field-pieces, wandered into poisoned-arrow country, fell into an ambush, and were shot down to a man. An expedition was sent up the Atrato to find the Golden Temple of Dabaiba, but here too the Indians had the advantage. Being naked and good swimmers, they easily dived under and upset the canoes. Half the Spaniards were drowned, and Balboa, who was second in command, brought the rest back to Antigua. And though many other expeditions were later sent up the Atrato, none has ever reached Dabaiba, so the golden temple must be there today—if it ever was there at all.

PIECES OF EIGHT.

Pedrarias, filled with fury at these defeats, took the field himself, but soon came down with a fever. Finally his alcalde, Espinosa, hurled himself with a sufficiently large force on the exhausted tribes and, by the beginning of 1517, established a Roman peace.

In the meanwhile, Balboa had been sent a royal commission as Adelantado of the South Seas, and Viceroy of the Pacific side of the Isthmus, but the jealous Pedrarias had held it up. Now Fonseca, the bishop, patched up a truce between the two. Balboa agreed to put away his Indian wife, and became engaged to the daughter of Pedrarias.

There was a place on the Atlantic shore, between Antigua and abandoned Santa Cruz, called by the Indians Acla, or "the Bones of Men," because two warlike chiefs of long ago had caused a great slaughter of their subjects there. Here Balboa cut down and shaped the timbers of four brigantines. These were carried by hundreds of Indians and a few negroes, over a rough trail to the headwaters of the Savannah River, down which they were rafted to the Gulf of San Miguel. It was an incredible piece of labor for the time, and none could have accomplished it but Nuñez de Balboa. When they came to set up the vessels, half the wood was found to be worm-eaten, and high tides and floods swept away much of the rest. But he persevered, until at last four fully equipped brigantines floated at anchor on the South Sea.

Then came word of a new governor sent from Spain to take the place of Pedrarias. Balboa confided to a friend that it might be wise for him to sail at once for Peru, "if this newcomer meant aught of ill to his lord Pedrarias." Now this false friend had been his rival for the love of the Indian girl, and revenged himself by denouncing Balboa to Pedrarias as a traitor. Francisco Pizarro was at once sent to arrest him, and, after a mockery of a trial, Vasco Nuñez de Balboa, Adelantado of the South Sea, and noblest of the conquistadores, died on the scaffold in the plaza of Acla.

Fearing the wrath of the new governor, Pedrarias crossed the Isthmus, and in 1519, founded a city on the site of a little fishing village called Panama. This name signifies, in the Indian language, "a place abounding in fish," and one reason the Spaniards settled here was to escape the famines they had suffered at Antigua. Both that town and Acla were soon abandoned to the Indians, who even now forbid white men to stay overnight in that region under penalty of death, so well do they still remember the cruelties of Pedrarias.

I wish I could add that vengeance overtook that wicked old man, but he lived to rule and do evil, both in Panama and in Nicaragua, until he was ninety years old. The new governor died suddenly, and several in authority that came after him, including one bishop of Panama, were poisoned by Pedrarias. As for the Indians he caused to be killed, the historian Oviedo declares them to have been more than two million.

The only consolation we have is the knowledge that Pedrarias, who was even fonder of gold than of bloodshed, was at first a partner of Pizarro's, when the man who had arrested Balboa sailed on his ships to the conquest of Peru; but later, Pedrarias lost his courage, and sold his quarter-share in the adventure for a miserable thousand crowns. How it must have wrung the cruel old miser's heart to see the ship loads of silver and gold that came up from the mines of Peru, to be carried across the Isthmus on the way to Spain. For it was this treasure-trade with Peru that made the wealth and glory of Old Panama.

CHAPTER VI
HOW SIR FRANCIS DRAKE RAIDED THE ISTHMUS

Sixty years after Balboa's discovery of the Pacific, the first Englishman to see that ocean looked at it from the top of a "goodlie and great high tree," somewhere in the jungle back of Old Panama. This man was Francis Drake, a bold sea-captain of Devon, who had come to the Isthmus to pay a debt he had long owed the Spaniards: a debt of revenge for treacherous wrong.

Five years before, in 1568, an English fleet under Sir John Hawkins had entered the harbor of San Juan de Ulloa (now Vera Cruz), in Mexico, ready either to trade peacefully with the Spaniards, or, if the latter preferred, to fight. The Spaniards received them as friends, exchanged hostages as evidence of good faith, waited until a very much larger Spanish fleet had come in, and then suddenly attacked the English with both ships and forts. After an all-day's fight, every English ship but two was captured, sunk, or ablaze; but the *Minion* of Hawkins, and Francis Drake's *Judith* fought their way out and carried the news to England. Queen Elizabeth could not go to war with Spain, then the mightiest power on earth, but she winked her royal eye at the private acts of her seamen.

Drake first made two quiet voyages to the Isthmus, to learn how the Spaniards handled the treasure-trade from Peru, and how he could best attack it. It is said that Drake even lived for a while in disguise at Nombre de Dios, which had been resettled and made the Atlantic port in 1519, the same year as the founding of Old Panama. A roughly paved way, called the Royal Road, had been built between the two cities by the forced labor of captive Indians, and over this in the dry season long trains of pack-mules carried the gold and silver that was brought up by sea from Peru to Panama, across the Isthmus to Nombre de Dios. During the nine months of the rainy season the route was over a better road from Panama to the little town of Venta Cruz, now called Cruces, at the head of navigation on the Chagres River, and down this river in flat-boats and canoes to the sea. Once a year a fleet of galleons came from Spain, bringing European goods for the colonists and carrying away the treasure that had been accumulating since the last trip in the King's treasure-house at Nombre de Dios. The English called this the "Plate Fleet," from the Spanish word *plata*, or silver.

Nombre de Dios was a ragged little town mostly bamboo huts and board shacks, except for the King's treasure-house, which was "very strongly built of lime and stone." The place was so unhealthy that it was known as "The Grave of the Spaniard," and most of the citizens spent the rainy season at Panama or Cruces, and only returned to Nombre de Dios to do business when the plate-fleet was in.

Drake learned all these things after two years' prowling up and down the coast, so in 1572 he made a third voyage to the Isthmus to put this knowledge to practical effect. Sailing boldly into Nombre de Dios harbor, at three o'clock in the morning on the twenty-ninth of July, Drake tumbled ashore with seventy-three men and captured the sea-battery before the Spaniards could fire a single one of its six brass guns. Dismounting these, the English marched into the plaza, with drums beating, trumpets sounding, and six "fire-pikes" or torches lighting the way with a lurid glare. There was a volley of shot from the Spanish musketeers, an answering flight of English arrows, a rush, a brief, brisk hand-to-hand fight, and the defenders went flying through the landward gate and down the road to Panama.

In the governor's house the English found a stack of solid silver bars, seventy feet long, ten wide, and twelve high, worth more than five million dollars but too heavy to carry away. So they went to the King's treasure-house for the gold and jewels stored there. "I have brought you to the mouth of me treasury of the world!" cried Drake, and ordered them to break in the door. But an instant later, he fell fainting from loss of blood, for during the fight in the plaza he had received a great wound in the thigh, which he had kept concealed until then. And you can realize how much his men loved Francis Drake, when in spite of his commands they left the treasure to get their wounded captain back to the boats. The garrison and citizens were rallying, and more troops had just come from Panama, but all the English got safely off, except one of the trumpeters.

"NOMBRE DE DIOS"—STREET SCENE.

SIR FRANCIS DRAKE.
Born in Devonshire, about 1540; died off Porto Bello, in 1596.

For the next six months Drake raided impudently up and down the coast, even capturing a ship in the harbor of Cartagena, the capital city of the Spanish Main, and the Spaniards dared not attack him. Then, when his wound was healed, and the dry season had come, he set out with eighteen Englishmen and thirty Cimaroons from his secret camping-place on the Atlantic shore to cross the Isthmus. The Cimaroons were some of the many negroes who had been brought to the Isthmus as slaves, to take the place of the almost exterminated Indians, but had escaped from their Spanish masters into the jungle. Here they intermarried with the Indians, built towns of their own, and defied the Spaniards. Bands of Cimaroons, armed with bows and spears,—firearms were above their understanding—roamed the forest or raided pack-trains on the Royal Road. And this was what they were now helping Drake to do, as for centuries afterwards, both Cimaroons and Indians helped every enemy of Spain that came their way.

The galleons from Spain were at Nombre de Dios, waiting for the pack-trains to bring across the treasure from the other plate-fleet from Peru, that Drake saw riding at anchor in the harbor of Panama. He had not enough men to go near the city, but as soon as they had seen the Pacific from the "goodlie and great high tree" Drake and his comrade, John Oxenham, both took oath that they would some day sail an English ship on that sea.

A Cimaroon, sent into the city as a spy, brought out the news that three pack-trains were to leave

Panama that night, traveling by moonlight to escape the heat, and laden, one with provisions, one with silver, and one with gold and jewels. A carefully planned ambush was laid on either side of the Royal Road, not far from Venta Cruz, but a silly sailor, named Robert Pike, spoiled everything by jumping up to look at a Spaniard who came riding out from the town. This horseman warned the train-escort, who sent forward the mules loaded with provisions. When Drake captured these, he knew the treasure-train had escaped him, so he charged into Venta Cruz to see what he could find there. But there was no treasure in the village, only some Spanish ladies who were dreadfully frightened, until Drake assured them that no woman or unarmed man had ever been harmed by him.

NATIVES PREPARING RICE FOR DINNER—
NOMBRE DE DIOS.

When he had returned to the Atlantic side of the Isthmus, Drake joined forces with some English freebooters, and they laid another ambush on the Royal Road, this time only a mile out of Nombre de Dios. At dawn, a string of a hundred and ninety mules came tinkling and pattering along from Panama, with an escort of forty-five Spanish soldiers. A volley dropped the lead-mules, the rest promptly lay down, and the escort broke and ran to Nombre de Dios, leaving Drake's men the richer by fifteen tons of gold and as much silver. The latter they buried round about, in the holes of the land-crabs, and it is said that the Spaniards were never able to find it, and that it must be there today. As for the gold, Drake divided it fairly, and sailed back to England with his share.

Two years later, in 1575, John Oxenham returned to the Isthmus, crossed it with the aid of the Cimaroons, built and launched a pinnace on the southern side, and was the first Englishman to sail the Pacific. How he raided the Pearl Islands and was captured and put to death by the Spaniards from Panama, you can read best in Kingsley's noble story of "Westward Ho!"

SAN BLAS INDIAN SQUAWS IN NATIVE DRESS.
Note the gold nose-rings.

It was left for Drake to enter this sea that Spain had claimed for her own, through the strait Magellan had found in 1520, and to be the next after him to sail round the world. How, with one little ship, the *Golden Hind*, Drake swept the west coast of South America, and took the great treasure-galleon *Cacafuego* a hundred and fifty leagues from Panama; how with a fleet he took and burned the city of Santo Domingo (but spared the cathedral because it held the ashes of Christopher Columbus), and sacked Cartagena; how with Sir John Hawkins he wiped out the memory of San Juan de Ulloa in the great Armada fight; how he won knighthood and "singed the King of Spain's beard," are all parts of another noble story for which there is no room here.

The dream of Drake's life was to capture the city of Panama. In 1595, he brought a fleet to the Isthmus with Sir John Hawkins, captured and burned Nombre de Dios, and landed seven hundred and fifty soldiers to march across to Panama. But the Spaniards had barricaded the Royal Road too strongly, and, besides, a great deal of sickness broke out on the fleet. So the English gave it up, and set sail for Columbus's old port of Porto Bello, but before they reached this harbor their admiral was dead.

They buried him a league from shore, and as the leaden coffin sank beneath the waves, the guns of the fleet roared a farewell broadside, and a fort that the Spaniards had built to defend their new town of Porto Bello was given to the flames. This was on the twenty-eighth of January, 1596. Some people declare that "Francis Drake lies buried in Nombre Dios bay"; but those who did the burying say Porto Bello. And Captain William Parker, who captured that town only six years later,—in spite of its fine new forts,—marks on his chart a spot not far outside the harbor as "the Place where my Shippes roade, being the rock where Sir Francis Drake his Coffin was throwne overboorde."

CHAPTER VII

HOW MORGAN THE BUCANEER SACKED OLD PANAMA

There are three sundry places where this citie (Old Panama) may without difficulty be taken, and spoyled by the Pirates. . . . And forasmuch as the most part of these people (the citizens) are marchants, they will not fight, but onely keepe their owne persons in safetie, and save their goods; as it hath bene sene heretofore in other places of these Indies. . . . Therefore it behooveth your majestie to fortifie these places very strongly."

So wrote Baptista Antonio, an Italian surveyor who had been sent by Philip II of Spain to report on his cities in the West Indies in 1587. Of the three ways he mentioned by which pirates could come to attack Old Panama, one was through the Darien country to the east, and nothing was done to prevent it. The second was by way of Nombre de Dios, but that town was already being abandoned for Porto Bello, healthier and strongly fortified with stone castles. The third route was up the Chagres, and the King did build a small wooden castle, called Fort San Lorenzo, to protect the mouth of the river. But nothing was done at Old Panama.

Yet with a little strengthening here and there, it could have been made a formidable place to attack. The sea protected it on the south with a broad belt of quicksands at low tide; on the west lay a marshy creek crossed by a narrow stone arch; and on the north or landward side was a swamp, drained by another stream (also crossed by a stone bridge, recently discovered) that flowed into the harbor on the east.

GALLEON

The space so enclosed was fourteen hundred and twelve varas (yards) from east to west, by four hundred and eighty-seven from north to south, and the city had only seven streets running up from the sea, and four along the beach. There were three plazas, on the largest of which stood the Cabildo or city hall, court house, jail, hospital, and other public buildings, which were of stone, and the cathedral, which at first was made of wood, like all the private houses. Scattered about the city were three small monasteries and a convent, and on a rocky knoll by the harbor stood the barracks of the Genoese company that traded in negro slaves.

These slaves were very numerous. In 1575, fifty-six years after the foundation of the city, there were only four hundred houses and five hundred Spanish citizens in the place, but the blacks and mulattoes numbered over three thousand. They drove the mules on the Royal Road, manned the flat-boats on the Chagres, cultivated the few fields and gardens; in short, did all the work while their masters made money in trade and speculation.

It was not so much the treasure-trade with Peru that brought wealth to the citizens of Old Panama, for that was a royal monopoly that profited only the king—and the officials that handled it. Neither was it the pearls from the Pearl Islands, nor the gold from the struggling placer-mines in Veragua. For a short time there was a profitable trade with the Philippines, soon stopped by a foolish royal decree. But what really profited the Isthmian merchants was the trade in smuggled goods.

Foreigners were strictly forbidden to trade with the Spanish colonies, and when the yearly plate-fleet came to Porto Bello, it was supposed to bring only homemade goods. But Spain has never been a great manufacturing country, and the company which had the monopoly of that trade usually sent only one small ship load. So when each of the other vessels sent ashore her sails to make a great booth for the busy weeks of the "Galleon Fair," there were more things sold than ever saw Spain or paid duty to the king. Every once in a while, the Spanish government would make an attempt to stop this free-trading by savagely attacking the foreign traders. So they had stirred up Sir Francis Drake against them, and now they were to rouse the bucaneers.

These were men of all nations, but principally English, French, and Dutch, who made a living hunting the wild cattle, descendants of stock introduced by the first Spanish discoverers, in the West Indian islands. They cured or dried the beef over a bed of live coals, after a fashion taught them by the Indians, and called by the French *boucan*, and from this they became known as the "boucaniers" or "bucaneers." When the Spaniards tried to drive them away by killing off the wild cattle, these fierce cowboys of the sea began to hunt the Spaniards. Paddling up astern of a becalmed galleon in their dug-out canoes, the bucaneers would put an ounce ball from one of their long, heavy muskets into every head that showed at a port-hole or over the rail; then, wedging the rudder fast, they would swarm on board with knife and cutlass. Soon they were capturing Spanish ships of war and cities, and they helped the British government under Cromwell turn the island of Jamaica from a Spanish into an English colony. The city of Port Royal, in that island, became their headquarters, and it was from there that they followed Henry Morgan to Porto Bello and Old Panama.

Henry Morgan was the son of a Welsh farmer. He ran away to sea as a boy, joined the bucaneers, and by his great skill both as a sailor and a fighter, became their leader. Like Sir Francis Drake's, his exploits are too many to be told here, but unlike Drake, who was of a noble and generous nature and fought like an honorable soldier, Harry Morgan was a greedy, bloodthirsty pirate. His men hated him, but they followed him, for he always led them to victory.

Sailing quietly up to a spot near Porto Bello, one dark night in 1669, Morgan landed with four hundred and sixty bucaneers, and before the garrison could take alarm, the town and all the castles but one were in his hands. This last fort was defended valiantly, from dawn till noon, when Morgan forced some captured priests and nuns to place scaling-ladders against the wall, knowing the Spaniards would not fire on them. So the bucaneers captured the fort and put all within it to the sword, the brave commander having refused to accept quarter. After plundering the city and torturing the inhabitants, Morgan sailed away; but first he answered the governor of Panama, who sent a man under a flag of truce, to ask him with what sort of weapons his men had captured so strong a city. Morgan gave the messenger a pistol and a few small bullets, as a sample or "slender pattern," with the word that he would himself come to Panama and take them back within a twelvemonth.

A BUCANEER.

Next year the advance forces of the bucaneers, four hundred strong, under Captain Bradley, landed near the mouth of the Chagres and attacked Fort San Lorenzo. Here double walls of palisades, filled in with earth, ran round the top of a steep hill. Outside was a ditch, inside were heavy cannon and a picked garrison of Spanish regulars. They beat off the first assaults with great loss to the bucaneers, one of whom was shot through the body by an

Indian bowman in the fort. Pulling out the arrow, the plucky pirate wrapped a bit of cotton round it, rammed it into his musket and fired it back. Set on fire by the powder, the burning arrow fell on a palm-thatched roof, and before the Spaniards could put it out, the powder-magazine had exploded and the castle was all ablaze. As the palisades burned, the earthworks crumbled into the ditch, and the bucaneer marksmen easily picked off the soldiers from the darkness of the jungle. When Fort San Lorenzo was stormed next morning, not a single officer and only thirty soldiers, twenty of whom were badly wounded, were left alive out of a garrison of three hundred and fourteen men. No place was ever defended more gallantly.

Morgan came in with his fleet and after placing garrisons both here and at Porto Bello, he started up the Chagres River with a picked force of fourteen hundred men. Very foolishly, they took only enough provisions to last two days. The Spaniards retreated before them, devastating the country, and for nine terrible days the bucaneers struggled on, eating their leather belts, grass, leaves, or anything that would fill their stomachs. Two hundred died of starvation or were shot by hostile Indians, but the rest won through to the hill, called ever since the "Hill of the Bucaneers," from which they caught their first glimpse of Old Panama.

ARMS OF THE OLD CITY OF
PANAMA.

Granted by royal decree, September 15th, 1521. In 1581, the
city was given the title of "Very noble and very loyal."

The city had been steadily growing until 1640, when it contained seven hundred and fifty houses with eight thousand inhabitants, about a quarter of whom were white. Four years later, a great fire destroyed most of the town, including the cathedral, and if we make no allowance for this setback, the former rate of increase would give us, by the end of 1670, about ten thousand inhabitants, and a thousand houses of all sorts. Among these was a splendid new stone cathedral, dedicated only five years before Morgan came.

For the defense of the city, the governor, Don Juan Perez de Guzman, mustered a force of four hundred cavalry, and twenty-four infantry companies of one hundred men each. This must have called out virtually every able-bodied white man and free mulatto and negro in Old Panama, for they could not have armed the slaves without turning them into Cimaroons. The best of the regular troops had been lost at Fort San Lorenzo, and the bulk of de Guzman's force was raw militia, many of the infantry being armed with fowling-pieces or shotguns.

Opposed to them were twelve hundred veteran fighting-men, no longer weak with hunger, for the Spaniards stupidly let a herd of cattle stray in their enemies' path, and the bucaneers had a great feast and a good night's rest before the battle. An Indian guide led them away from the ambuscades and batteries placed on the Royal Road, forcing de Guzman to attack the English on the open plain before the city. The battle began at sunrise on the twenty-eighth of January, 1671.

The Spanish cavalry charged impetuously, but the bucaneer marksmen coolly shot half the squadron out of their saddles at the first volley, and soon scattered the rest, though they rallied again and again. An attempt was made to drive a herd of two thousand wild bulls over the bucaneers, who easily stampeded them in every direction. Nothing was left but the huddled mass of Spanish foot soldiers, inferior both at long range and hand-to-hand fighting, but brave enough to stand their ground until six hundred of them were killed. Then they broke and fled into the city.

De Guzman, after vainly trying to rally his defeated troops, blew up the powder-magazines, which started fires all over the city. To make it worse, many houses were set on fire by revengeful negro and Indian slaves. By the time Morgan's men had stormed the batteries that defended the bridges, a strong sea breeze was sweeping the flames through the town. Both the bucaneers and the citizens tried to stop the fire, blowing up some of the houses in its path and tearing down others, but by the next morning, Old Panama was a heap of ashes.

Morgan camped in the ruins for a month, torturing prisoners and hunting for treasure. He found much less than he expected, for a galleon had escaped to sea with all that belonged to the church and the king. After plundering the islands and all the country round, and receiving ransom for their prisoners, the bucaneers returned to Fort San Lorenzo. Here that old villain Morgan got the treasure on board his own ship and sailed away, leaving his comrades in the lurch. With this doubly stolen money, he not only bought a pardon from King Charles II, but became Sir Henry Morgan, lieutenant-governor of Jamaica, and a most merciless catcher and hanger of bucaneers!

Among the men deserted by Morgan was Jan Esquemeling, a Dutchman, who wrote a most entertaining book on "The Bucaneers of America." In it he declares that Old Panama contained two thousand richly furnished mansions, besides five thousand smaller houses. Now Esquemeling never entered the city until it was already on fire, and to any one acquainted with the facts, this part of his narrative reads like a boasting pirate's yarn, smacking strongly of Sindbad the Sailor. Yet on the strength of it, modern historians have credited Old Panama with a population of from thirty to fifty thousand and luxury

That far

Outshone the wealth of Ormus and of Ind.

But the Spanish chroniclers make no mention of any such amazing growth after the fire of 1644; and the recent excavations made on the site by the Panamanian government show no ruins outside the quadrangle of fourteen hundred and twelve by four hundred and eighty-seven yards enclosed by the sea and the two creeks. Inside that space there is not room for seven thousand huts, let alone houses, after you allow for eleven streets, three plazas, and a sizable cathedral. Today, the vine-clad shell of that cathedral's tower, the stone arches of two bridges, and a few bits of jungle-smothered wall, are all that mark the spot where stood the proud city of Old Panama.

CHAPTER VIII
HOW THE ENGLISH FAILED TO TAKE NEW PANAMA

Two years after the destruction of Old Panama, the city was rebuilt on a better site, six miles to the west. Here, on a rocky peninsula at the foot of Ancon Hill it received even better protection from shoals and coral reefs than at the former place, and was much nearer the islands of Naos and Taboga, that had always been the port for vessels of any size. These natural defenses were strengthened by stone walls so massive and well-armed with heavy cannon that they cost, even with slave labor, over eleven million dollars. "I am looking for those expensive walls of Panama," said the King of Spain, when asked why he stood gazing out of a palace window to the west. "They cost enough to be visible from here."

But those costly walls were to earn their keep, for they alone kept the bucaneers from overrunning Panama, and making it another Jamaica. Only seven years after Morgan left the Isthmus, the town of Porto Bello was plundered by a small gang of bucaneers, the garrison not daring to come out of the forts. Other raiders had already gone through the Straits of Magellan, but the favorite route of these later bucaneers was through the Darien region, by the same pass used by Balboa. The Darien Indians, glad to ally themselves with any enemies of their ancient foes, the Spaniards, guided across large parties both of English and French bucaneers, under many different captains, but all with the same purpose, of plundering the Spaniards in the South Seas. Between 1680 and 1688, these daring raiders had wiped out every settlement and mining-camp on the Pacific shore of Darien, plundered every island, defeated two Spanish fleets in the Bay of Panama, and fought a drawn battle with a third, and were only kept out of the city by its strong walls.

SEA WALL, PANAMA CITY

Among these later bucaneers were not a few well-educated men, like Captain Dampier, who carefully studied the natural history of the Isthmus, and made some excellent maps. Lionel Wafer, surgeon on one of the ships, lived for months among the Darien Indians, learned their language, and wrote a long book about them when he returned to England. Several of the captains were discussing the idea of forming a colony among these friendly Indians, and inviting all old bucaneers to come and settle there. This project was stopped, and the alliance between the English and French bucaneers broken off by England's becoming the ally of Spain against France, after the Revolution of 1688. At the same time a pardon was offered to all bucaneers who ceased making private war on Spain, and those that persisted were thereafter to be treated as pirates.

The idea of starting a colony in Darien, reopening the road between Acla and the Gulf of San Miguel, and establishing a transisthmian trade between Europe and Asia, appealed to James Patterson, a shrewd Scotch financier, who had already founded the Bank of England. His scheme met with instant approval in Scotland, then a distinct kingdom, though under the same monarch as England. The royal approval having been given to an act of the Scottish Parliament, incorporating a company for the purpose of founding such a colony, the Scotch enthusiastically declared,

King William did encourage us, against the English will;
His word is like a stately oak, will neither bend nor break,
We 'll venture life and fortune both for Scotland and his sake.

But there was very little of the "stately oak" about William Ill's behavior, when the powerful British East India Company complained that its monopoly of trade with the East might be injured. At once, the governors of Jamaica and all other

English colonies were forbidden to help the Scotch colonists, a warship was sent to seize the land if possible, before they disembarked, and, heaviest blow of all, the English subscribers were made to return their shares. So though the Scotch went ahead by themselves, reached Darien before the English warship, and established their colony, they had not enough money to maintain it properly.

The Indians were glad to welcome twelve hundred white men, come, as they supposed, to wage war on the Spaniards. A harbor near Balboa's old town of Acla was now named Caledonia Bay, and on it was built the town of New Edinburgh, guarded by Fort St. Andrew. A treaty of alliance was made with the Indians, who were eager to take the field, and great apprehension was felt at Panama and Porto Bello.

But to the astonishment of every one else, the Scotch did nothing but sit still, until a quarter of them had died of starvation and fever. Then the rest took ship to New York, in June, 1699, eight months after the founding of the colony, and when reinforcements were already on the way. The second expedition only left a few men and sailed away, but the third brought thirteen hundred more. Ship loads of food came from several of the English colonies in North America, in spite of the King's command, but there was no money in New Edinburgh to buy it. Neither was there enough sense among the wrangling ministers and whisky-soaked counselors to realize that if they did not attack the Spaniards while the Scotchmen were still healthy, the Spaniards would certainly attack them after they were sick. Presently a small Spanish force marched against New Edinburgh, but were routed out of their palisaded camp by half their number of Scots under Captain Campbell. But when a strong fleet from Cartagena attacked the town there were very few healthy men left in it, and the colonists were glad to accept the generous terms offered and leave the country. So weak were most of them that the Spaniards had to help them hoist their sails.

So ended the attempt to plant a colony in Darien. It failed for two reasons: the lack of a leader among the Scotch, and the short-sighted jealousy of the English. It was no love of Spain, who had ceased to be her ally, but selfish fear for her own trade, that set England's face against the struggling Scotch colony. Had it been kept alive only a few years longer, until the War of the Spanish Succession, New Edinburgh and its Indian allies would have made it easy for England to take not only Darien but the whole Isthmus of Panama. Later, England realized the truth of Patterson's statement that, "These doors of the seas, and the keys of the universe, would be capable of enabling their possessors to give laws to both oceans, and to become the arbitrators of the commercial world."

When England had her next war with Spain, "The War of Jenkins's Ear," Admiral Edward Vernon, after whom Washington's home, Mt. Vernon, is named, was sent to attack Porto Bello. With six ships of the line he battered down its stone castles, captured the town, and sank some Spanish *guarda-costas* or revenue-cutters, including the one whose captain had cut off the ear of Captain Jenkins, an English trader, and so started the war. This was in 1739. Next year Vernon captured the present stone castle of San Lorenzo, that had replaced the wooden one destroyed by Morgan, and prepared to send a force across the Isthmus to attack New Panama, against which another fleet, under Admiral Anson, had been sent round the Horn. But Vernon's men began to die of fevers, and he feared to advance without cannon, which could not be taken either up the Chagres or along the Royal Road; so he attacked Cartagena instead, failed there, and went home. Hearing this, Anson sailed away to attack Manila, and Panama was saved.

Only the shell of its former greatness was saved, however, for all these wars had driven trade away from the Isthmus to the Straits of Magellan. Moreover, the Peruvian mines were nearly exhausted, and after the middle of the eighteenth century, the plate fleets sailed no more from Porto Bello. Both Spain and England turned their attention away from Panama to Nicaragua, and, in 1780, Horatio Nelson, then a post-captain, was sent to take that country for George III. But though he easily defeated the Spaniards, Nelson was driven away by yellow fever, that killed one hundred and ninety out of the two hundred men on his ship.

RENTED GRAVES, CEMETERY, PANAMA CITY.

So, for one reason or another, from the time when the Isthmus lay helpless under the feet of Morgan until the last of the Spanish viceroys drove a band of English filibusters out of the oft-captured town of Porto Bello, in 1819, the English failed to take Panama from Spain. "These doors of the seas and keys of the universe" were not destined to be theirs.

CHAPTER IX
HOW THE AMERICANS BUILT THE PANAMA RAILROAD

Panama was the last stronghold, as it had been the first colony, of Spain in the three Americas, but when the Isthmus somewhat languidly declared its independence in 1821, the commander of the royal troops did not consider the former "Treasure-House of the World" worth the snap of a flint-lock. For since 1740, when trade had left it for the Cape Horn route, Panama had withered up into a place of almost no importance. Now that the old Spanish prohibition of foreign trade was removed, the Isthmus expected to share with the rest of Spanish America in a great commercial revival.

But though foreign ships now came to the village at the mouth of the Chagres, for which Porto Bello was presently abandoned, the difficulty of getting their cargoes across the Isthmus was too great. Many schemes were advanced for building a horse-car line or digging a canal, but nothing ever came of them. Year after year, the torpid little community lay between its two oceans and "drowsed the long tides idle," till it woke to new life with the discovery of gold in California, and the coming of the Forty-niners.

Thousands of Americans were poled and paddled up the Chagres in overcrowded dugouts to Cruces, and rode over the old paved road, now no better than a worn-out trail, to Panama City. So rough was the road that the mules could scarcely scramble over it, and many passengers preferred to be carried in chairs on the backs of negro or Indian porters. Four nights were usually spent on the journey across the Isthmus, nights of crowded discomfort in native huts, where hammocks were rented for two dollars, and eggs cost twenty-five cents apiece. Panama was crammed with red-shirted Americans, who often waited months for a ship to take them to San Francisco, where ships were rotting three-deep at the wharves, while their crews went gold-hunting. To pass the time, the Yankees scratched their names on the ramparts of the sea-wall, and started two papers, the *Star* and the *Herald*, which, after a brief rivalry, combined in the present *Panama Star and Herald*, a daily, printed in both Spanish and English. Trade boomed, brigandage flourished, and there was more hiring of mules, renting of lodgings, raising of prices, and fleecing of strangers, than the Isthmus had seen since the roaring days of the Galleon Fair.

From Harper's Magazine, by special permission of the publishers.

SURVEYING FOR THE PANAMA RAILROAD IN 1850.

As soon as California and Oregon had been taken into the Union, Congress had authorized a line of steamers to be run down either coast to the Isthmus, and had appropriated money to pay them for carrying the United States mail. Mr. William H. Aspinwall, who had secured the line on the Pacific side, and Mr. George Law, who had that on the Atlantic, combined with a third New York capitalist, Mr. Henry Chauncey, to build a railroad across the Isthmus. Chauncey and John L. Stephens, an experienced Central American traveler, had already obtained from the government of the Republic of New Granada, of which Panama was now a state, the exclusive right to build such a road; and Stephens had explored the route with a skilled engineer, Mr. J. L. Baldwin, and reported that it could be built at a profitable cost.

The Panama Railroad Company was accordingly incorporated, with a New York charter and a capital of a million dollars, and the construction of the road entrusted to two experienced contractors, Colonel Totten and Mr. Trautwine. But no sooner had they reached the Isthmus than they found that the "gold-rush," now fairly begun, had so raised the local prices of labor and materials that they begged the company to release them from the contract. This was done, and they were retained as engineers of the company, which proceeded to build the road itself.

From Harper's Magazine, by special permission of the publishers.
PANAMA RAILROAD IN 1855.

A later survey by Baldwin and Colonel Hughes, who had been detailed from the United States Topographical Corps, had located the Pacific terminus at Panama City, and the Atlantic end at Navy or Limon Bay, between the mouth of the Chagres and Porto Bello. On Manzanillo Island in this bay, some time in the month of May, 1850, Trautwine and Baldwin struck the first blow.

"No imposing ceremony inaugurated the breaking ground. Two American citizens, leaping, ax in hand, from a native canoe upon a wild and desolate island, their retinue consisting of half a dozen Indians, who clear the path with rude knives, strike their glittering axes into the nearest tree; the rapid blows reverberate from shore to shore, and the stately cocoa crashes upon the beach. Thus unostentatiously was announced the commencement of a railway, which, from the interests and difficulties involved, might well be looked upon as one of the grandest and boldest enterprises ever attempted."

Space was cleared for the erection of a storehouse, but so unhealthy was the low, swampy coral island, awash at high tide, and breeding swarms of malaria-spreading mosquitos, that the force were obliged to live on the two-hundred ton brig that had brought them and their supplies from New York. When Colonel Totten and Mr. Stephens, who had been made president of the company, arrived with more laborers from Cartagena, the little brig became uncomfortably overcrowded, and was replaced with the hull of a condemned steamer, the *Telegraph*, brought round from the mouth of the Chagres.

"Surveys of the island and adjacent country were now pushed vigorously forward. It was in the depth of the rainy season, and the working parties, in addition to being constantly drenched from above, were forced to wade in from two to four feet of mud and water, over the mangrove swamps and tangled vines of the imperfect openings cut by the natives, who, with their machetes, preceded them to clear the way. Then, at night, rated and exhausted, they dragged themselves back to their quarters on the *Telegraph*, to toss until morning among the pitiless insects. Numbers were daily taken down with fever; and, notwithstanding that the whole working party was changed weekly, large accessions were constantly needed to keep up the required force. The works were alternately in charge of Messrs. Totten and Baldwin, one attending to the duty while the other recuperated from his last attack of fever."

FRENCH LOCOMOTIVES AND MACHINES
Left to rust in the jungle, near Empire.

So they drove the line, over a trestle to the mainland, through the marshy lowlands to firmer ground at Mount Hope or Monkey Hill, then half built, half floated it over the deep Black Swamp to the banks of the Chagres at Gatun. A couple of ship loads of materials had been brought up the river to this point (now buried under the great dam) and by the first of October, 1851, the rails had been laid and working trains were running as far as Gatun. Two large passenger steamers, unable to cross the bar of the Chagres in a storm, were forced to put into Limon Bay, and their passengers, over a thousand in number, were only too glad to ride on flat-cars to Gatun and begin their river journey there.

When news of this unexpected passenger traffic reached New York, it sent up the value of the company's stock, which had fallen very low, for the original million dollars had been spent, and the road was far from completion. Now the steamers came reguarly to Navy Bay, where docks had been built, and a settlement had grown up as the island was cleared. Mr. Stephens proposed that this town be given the name of one of the founders of the railroad, and on the second of February, 1852, it became the city of Aspinwall. This name, however, was never recognized by the native authorities, who insisted on naming the place after Columbus, the discoverer of Limon Bay. Finally, after many years of trouble for the map-makers, the native government won the day by refusing to deliver any more mail addressed to "Aspinwall," and the city is now called Colon, as the Spaniards called Columbus.

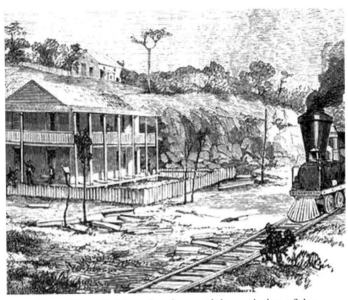

From Harper's Magazine, by special permission of the publishers.

GATUN STATION. Panama Railroad in 1855.

The road was pushed on along the bank of the Chagres to a place called Barbacoas, an Indian word meaning "bridge." And here a bridge three hundred feet long had to be built over a river that sometimes rose forty feet in a single night. About this time Mr. John L. Stephens died, and his successor tried the experiment of having the great bridge and the remainder of the line built by contract. But after a valuable year had been wasted, not a tenth had been completed, and the contractors were bankrupt. Releasing them, the company, under a third and stronger president, set out to finish the work itself.

Every effort was made to assemble a strong working force, and recruits were brought from the four corners of the earth. But northern whitemen are not made for pick and shovel labor in the tropics, and the hundreds of sturdy Irish and European peasants did little but die of heat and malaria. Much was expected from a thousand Chinese coolies, but they became so demoralized by the death of some of their number from fever, in this strange and terrible land, that they were seized with a passion for suicide, and scarcely two hundred left the Isthmus alive. Some work was done by coolies from India, but the best workmen were found to be negroes from Jamaica and other islands in the West Indies.

There is a popular fable, that will be told and believed as long as the Chagres runs to the sea, that the building of the Panama Railroad cost a life for every tie. But there were about a hundred and fifty thousand ties in the fifty miles of single track, and there have never been that many inhabitants on the Isthmus since Pedrarias the Cruel killed off the Indians. As a matter of fact and record, the total number employed, from the beginning of the work to the end, was about six thousand; and the number of deaths eight hundred and thirty-five. Doubtless many others sickened on the Isthmus, and died soon after they left it, but even so, the health of the force was remarkably good, for men toiling in a tropical swamp at a time when no doctor knew how to fight malaria and yellow fever. There was besides no cold storage to preserve the food, almost every mouthful of which had to be brought two thousand miles from New York.

A bridge of massive timbers was thrown across the Chagres at Barbacoas, and the road pushed on to the crest of the divide, at Culebra. In the meanwhile, men and materials had been shipped round the Horn, and eleven miles of track were laid from Panama to Culebra. Here, "on the twenty-seventh day of January, 1855, at midnight, in darkness and rain, the last rail was laid, and on the following day a locomotive passed from ocean to ocean."

From Harper's Magazine, by special permission of the publishers.
SAN PABLO STATION. Panama Railroad in 1855.

FRENCH DREDGES TIED UP TO THE BANK AFTER
THE COLLAPSE OF DE LESSEPS COMPANY.

But, though open, the railroad was far from being completed. Ravines were crossed on crazy trestles of green timber, the track was unballasted, and there was a great lack of both engines and cars. So the superintendent recommended that, until they were better able to handle traffic, most of it be kept away by charging the very high rates of fifty cents a mile for passengers, five cents a pound for baggage, and fifty cents a cubic foot for freight.

"To his surprise, these provisional rates were adopted; and, what is more, they remained in force for more than twenty years. It was found just as easy to get large rates as small; and thus, without looking very much to the future, this goose soon began to lay golden eggs with astonishing

105

extravagance. The road was put in good order, with track foremen established in neat cottages four or five miles apart, along the whole line. New engines and cars were put on, commodious terminal wharves and other buildings provided, and all things were in excellent shape." Trestles were made into solid embankments and wooden bridges replaced with iron; the great girder bridge at Barbacoas being the wonder of the time. Instead of pine, too quickly eaten up by ants, the ties were made of lignum-vitæ, so hard that holes had to be bored before the spikes could be driven. The telegraph poles were made of cement, molded round a pine scantling, a device that seems strangely modern.

Instead of one million dollars, the total cost of building this fifty-mile railroad was eight millions. But even before the first through track was laid, it had earned two million dollars' worth of fares, and during the first ten years of its existence, it took in $11,339,662.78. This was the Golden Age of the Panama Railroad, when it enjoyed the monopoly of the Atlantic trade, not only of California, but the entire west coast of the three Americas.

From Harper's Magazine, by special permission of the publishers.

TERMINUS AT PANAMA.

Panama Railroad in 1855.

Its stock earned dividends of twenty-four per cent, a year, and was considered one of the safest investments in Wall Street.

But in the contract made between John L. Stephens and the government of New Granada, that government had been given the right to buy the Panama Railroad, twenty years after it was opened, for five million dollars—and it was now paying twenty-four per cent, on seven million dollars' worth of stock! At the end of the twelfth year, Colonel Totten went to Bogotá, the capital, and succeeded in obtaining a new franchise for ninety-nine years, but at the heavy cost of a million down and two hundred and fifty thousand a year, with the additional obligation of extending the railroad to the islands in the Bay of Panama.

Two years later came the completion of the Union Pacific Railroad, and the loss of the California trade. But far more important than this was the traffic with the west coast of South and Central America, carried almost entirely by the ships of a British corporation, the Pacific Steam Navigation Company. The incredible stupidity of the Panama Railroad's directors forced this company to abandon its shops and dockyards on the Island of Taboga, in the Bay of Panama, and send its ships direct to England through the Straits of Magellan. Too late they saw that most of the trade went with them.

So, like Spain, the Panama Railroad built a trade-route across the Isthmus, monopolized it, flourished, and decayed. Its once-prized stock became the football of Wall Street speculators, its tracks the traditional "two streaks of rust." But unlike Spain's, its star was to rise again.

CHAPTER X
HOW THE FRENCH TRIED TO DIG THE CANAL

There is a large, iron steam-launch, used by our government to carry sick canal-workers to the sanatorium on Taboga Island, that was brought to the Isthmus by the French, but for a very different purpose. With two oceans to float it in, they stuck this launch high and dry at the bottom of the unfinished Gaillard Cut, to the great astonishment of the Americans who found it there in 1904. It had been placed there, explained an old employee of the French company, and a trench dug round it, so that when the floods of the rainy season filled the trench, a clever photographer could take a picture showing "navigation through the Cut." Such a picture, when exhibited in Paris, would make people think the work was nearly finished, and that the money they had invested in it was well spent. It is a good illustration of how the French tried to dig the Canal.

From the beginning, the French Canal Company (known in full as "La Société Internationale du Canal Interoceanique") sailed a great many boats on dry land and made people believe they were afloat. They sent Lieutenant Lucien Napoleon Bonaparte Wyse of the French Navy, to make a survey of the Isthmus in 1877, and, though he never went more than two-thirds of the distance from Panama to

Colon, he brought back complete plans, with the cost of construction figured out to within ten per cent, for a sea-level canal between the two cities. After a little more work on the Isthmus, next year, Wyse obtained a concession from the government at Bogotá, granting the exclusive right to build an interoceanic canal, not only at Panama, but anywhere else through the territory of the United States of Colombia, as New Granada was then called. When we remember the thorough preliminary surveys made for the Panama Railroad by Stephens and Hughes and Baldwin, it seems incredible that the French people should have taken Wyse seriously, and invested hundreds of millions of dollars in an enterprise of which they knew so little. What blinded them was the name of the man who now came forward as the head of that enterprise, Ferdinand de Lesseps.

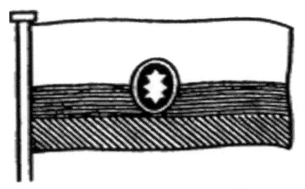

COLOMBIA NATIONAL FLAG.

He was "the great Frenchman," the most popular and honored man in France, because of the glory he had won her by the construction of the Suez Canal. Sent on a diplomatic mission to Egypt, de Lesseps, though not a trained engineer, had recognized the ease with which a ship canal could be cut through the hundred miles of level sand that separated the Mediterranean from the Red Sea. It took both imagination and courage to conceive a ship canal of that length, and the greatest difficulty, as with every new thing, lay in persuading people that it would not necessarily be a failure, because there had never been anything just like it before. The actual digging was as simple as making the moat round a sand castle at the seashore. A company was formed in France, the Khedive of Egypt took a majority of the stock, and forced thousands of his subjects to work as laborers for virtually nothing. The Suez Canal was completed in ten years, at a cost of a million dollars a mile, and ever since its opening in 1869 it has paid its owners handsome profits. But the bankrupt successor of the Khedive sold his stock to the British government, which has a very great interest in Suez because its ships must pass through there on the way to India, and today the English are the real rulers both of Egypt and the Suez Canal.

De Lesseps first appeared in connection with Panama as chairman of the International Canal Congress held in Paris in May, 1879. The experienced naval officers and trained engineers who were invited from many different countries, found themselves in a helpless minority. Their advice was not asked, and their presence had been sought merely to lend dignity and a show of authority to M. de Lesseps's decision, already made, to build a sea-level canal across the Isthmus of Panama according to the plans of Lieutenant Wyse. The chairman allowed no discussion of the advantages either of a lock canal at Panama, or of any kind of a canal at Nicaragua, but forced the adoption of the type and route he favored, by the vote of a small majority of French admirers, very few of whom were practical engineers. Then, adjourning his dummy congress, de Lesseps came forward as head of the French Canal Company, which had already paid Lieutenant Wyse $2,000,000 for his worthless surveys and valuable concessions. Finally, after everything had been decided on, de Lesseps went to the Isthmus with an imposing "Technical Commission" of distinguished engineers.

When President Roosevelt made his first inspection of the Panama Canal, nearly twenty-seven years afterwards, he went there in November, at the climax of the rainy season, because he wanted to see things at their worst. For exactly the opposite reason, de Lesseps chose December and January, when the rains have virtually ceased, and the country looks its prettiest. After one trip across the Panama Railroad, many speeches, and no end of feasting and drinking of healths, he hurried away to the United States, where he spent a great deal more time trying to induce the Americans to invest money in his enterprise, but without much success.

De Lesseps made another trip to the Isthmus in 1886.

Except for these two short visits, which together covered barely two months, de Lesseps never set foot in Panama, but attempted to dig the canal from his office in Paris. Few people realize that today, or that de Lesseps was born as long ago as 1805. He was more than seventy years old, and though he knew very little about technical engineering, his success at Suez and the praise of flatterers made him believe that he was the greatest engineer in the world. As he had dominated the Congress, so he ruled the Canal Company, absolutely and blindly. Ignoring the great differences between the level, rainless sands of one isthmus, and the rocky hills and flooded jungles of the other, de Lesseps declared that "the Panama Canal will be more easily begun, finished, and maintained than the Suez Canal." The proposed canal was to be a ditch dug down to twenty-seven and a half feet below sea-level, seventy-two feet wide at the bottom, and ninety at the water-line. In general, it was to follow the line of the Panama Railroad, from ocean to ocean. To keep the canal from being flooded by the Chagres, a great dam was to be built across that river at a place not far below Cruces, called Gamboa. Because of the difference between the tides of the two oceans, a large tidal basin was to be dug out of the swamps on the Pacific side, where the rise and fall is ten times that on the Atlantic.

COUNT DE LESSEPS IN 1880.

The Paris Congress thought that such a canal *might* be built for $214,000,000. The Technical Commission, after a few weeks on the Isthmus, said that it *could* be done for $168,600,000. Ferdinand de Lesseps, on his own responsibility, reduced these figures to $120,000,000, and declared that the Canal would be open in six years, and that enough ships would pass through in the first year after that to pay $18,000,000 worth of tolls. Allured by these figures, and trusting in the word of the "great Frenchman" hundreds of thousands of his countrymen invested their savings in the worthless stock of the Canal Company. But the only persons who made any money out of the enterprise were the swindlers and speculators who used the deluded old man's honored name as a bait for other people's money. De Lesseps himself was honest, but so blinded by the memory of his past success that he could see nothing in Panama but another Suez.

DREDGE ABANDONED BY THE FRENCH AND
REPAIRED BY THE AMERICANS.
The man in front of it did the job.

Thousands of laborers and millions of dollars' worth of machinery were sent to the Isthmus, before the slightest preparation had been made to receive them. The Panama Railroad refused to carry these men and materials except as ordinary passengers and freight, at its own high rates. This soon forced the French Canal Company to buy the railroad, paying for it, including termini, $25,000,000, or more than three times what it cost to build it. The organization and management of the road, however, still remained American.

This lack of foresight was the first great cause of the French failure, and the second was disease. From the beginning, yellow fever and malaria broke out in every labor camp, and attacked almost every engineer and workman, killing hundreds, and demoralizing the rest. At that time, no one knew how to prevent these diseases, but the French tried their best to cure those that fell sick. They built two splendid hospitals, one on terraces laid out on the side of Ancon Hill, overlooking the city of Panama, and the other on piles out over the water of Limon Bay at Colon. In these hospitals, the feet of the cots were placed in little pans of water to keep ants and other insects from crawling up, and no one noticed the mosquito "wrigglers" swarming in the stagnant water of these pans, or in the many ornamental bowls of flowers. But when a fever patient was brought into the hospital, the mosquitos bred there would suck the poison from his blood, and quickly spread it through the unscreened wards. Malaria means "bad air," and the French in Panama thought it was caused by the thick white mist that crept at night over the surface of the marshes, and men spoke with terror of this harmless fog and called it "Creeping Johnny." Every evening the Sisters of Charity who acted as nurses—good, pious women, but ignorant and untrained—would close all the doors and windows tight to keep out the terrible Creeping Johnny, and then leave their patients to spend the night without either attendance or fresh air. Too often there was more than one corpse to carry out in the morning.

No proper attention was paid to feeding the force, and there was altogether too little good food, and too much bad liquor. Such a combination is harmful enough anywhere, but in the tropics it is deadly. And there was no lack of other evils to make it deadlier.

"From the time that operations were well under way until the end, the state of things was like the life at 'Red Hoss Mountain,' described by Eugene Field,

> When the money flowed like likker . . . With the joints all throwed wide open 'nd no sheriff to demur!

"Vice flourished. Gambling of every kind, and every other form of wickedness were common day and night.

The blush of shame became virtually unknown. That violence was not more frequent will forever remain a wonder; but strange to say, in the midst of this carnival of depravity, life and property were comparatively safe. These were facts of which I was a constant witness."

This state of affairs naturally caused a great loss of life; exactly how great it is difficult to determine. As in the case of the building of the Panama Railroad, there has been much exaggeration and wild guessing. After careful research, the Secretary of the Isthmian Canal Commission estimated the

117

number of deaths among the French and their employees at from fifteen to twenty thousand.

The third great cause of the failure of the French Canal Company was graft. Everyone connected with it was extravagant, and very few except M. de Lesseps were honest. More money was spent in Paris than ever reached the Isthmus, and what did come was wasted on almost everything but excavation. The pay roll was full of the names of employees whose hardest work was to draw their salaries. "There is enough bureaucratic work and there are enough officers on the Isthmus to furnish at least one dozen first-class republics with officials for all their departments. The expenditure has been simply colossal. One director-general lived in a mansion that cost over $100,000; his pay was $50,000 a year, and every time he went out on the line he had fifty dollars a day additional. He traveled in a handsome Pullman car, specially constructed, which was reported to have cost some $42,000. Later, wishing a summer residence, a most expensive building was put up near La Boca (now Balboa). The preparation of the grounds, the building, and the roads thereto, cost upwards of $150,000."

When the Americans came to the Isthmus, they found three of these private Pullmans, on a railroad scarcely fifty miles long; a stableful of carriages, and acres of ornamental grounds, with avenues shaded by beautiful royal palms from Cuba. There was one warehouse full of what looked like wooden snow-shovels, but were probably designed for shoveling sand, which is not found on the canal line, and in another were several thousand oil torches for the parade at the opening of the Canal. When we consider these things, the wonder is, not that the French failed to dig the Canal, but that they dug as much as they did. Our army engineers speak very highly of their predecessors' plans and surveys. The French suffered, like the Scotch in Darien, from the lack of a leader, for there was usually a new chief engineer every six months, and the work was split up among six large contractors and many small ones. Though the engineers who directed the work were French, the two contractors who did most of the digging were not. It was a Dutch firm (Artigue, Sonderegger & Co.) that took a surprisingly large quantity of dirt out of the Gaillard Cut, with clumsy excavators that could only work in soft ground, and little Belgian locomotives and cars that look as if they came out of a toy-shop. The dredges and other floating equipment were much better, and many of them are still in use. Most of these dredges were built in Scotland. But it was an American firm (the American Dredging and Contracting Co.) that dredged the opening of the Canal from Colon to beyond Gatun. This company was the only contractor that made an honest profit out of the enterprise, and its big homemade, wooden dredges had cut fourteen miles inland, when the smash came in 1889.

FRENCH METHOD OF EXCAVATION IN THE
CULEBRA CUT.

Instead of the $120,000,000 originally asked for by M. de Lesseps, he had received and spent over $260,000,000. Instead of completing the Canal in six years, his company had dug less than a quarter of it in nine. Not a stone had been laid on the proposed great dam at Gamboa. Nothing had been done on the tidal basin except to discover that a few feet under what the Technical Commission had supposed to be an easily dredged swamp lay a solid ledge of hard rock. Year after year M. de Lesseps had kept explaining, and putting off the opening of the Canal, and asking for more money, until more had been spent than any possible traffic through the Canal could pay a profit on. Instead of finding Panama an easier task than Suez, the French had already dug 80,000,000 cubic yards, several million more than they did at Suez, and spent more than twice as much money. It was plain that the end had come. The French fled from the Isthmus, leaving it strewn as with the wreckage of a retreating army. Trains of dump cars stood rusting on sidings, or lay tumbled in heaps at the bottom of embankments. In one place, over fifty vine-covered locomotives can be counted at the edge of the jungle, from which the Americans dug out miles of narrow-gage track, cars, engines, and even a whole lost town. A lagoon near Colon was crammed with sunken barges and dredges. Others were abandoned at the Pacific entrance, or tied up to the banks of the Chagres, where the shifting of the river left some of them far inland. Thousands of Jamaican negroes who had worked on the Canal had no money with which to return home, and either went back to the West Indies at the expense of the British Government, or else built huts and settled down in the jungle.

A receiver was appointed for the French Canal Company, and a careful investigation made of its affairs. Criminal charges were brought against de Lesseps, who was convicted and sentenced to five years' imprisonment. But the sentence was never enforced against the old and broken-hearted man, and in a few months he died. Thousands of poor people were ruined. As for the real culprits, several committed suicide, and others were fined and imprisoned. Among those found guilty were so many senators, deputies, and other members of the French Government that for a short time there seemed danger of a revolution and the overturning of the Republic.

As most of the assets in the hands of the receiver consisted of the equipment and the work already done on the Isthmus, it was his duty to see that the enterprise was continued. So the French Government permitted the formation of the New Panama Canal Company out of the wreckage of the old one. This company took over all the machinery and buildings on the Isthmus, and in 1894 secured a concession from Colombia to finish the Canal in ten years.

The New Panama Canal Company went to work in the right way, and made most of the excellent surveys for which our engineers, who have found them extremely valuable, have given so much credit to their French predecessors. But the new company had so little money that it could keep only a few hundred men and two or three excavators busy in the Cut. It became plainer every year that the Canal could never be finished by 1904, and that the company's only hope was to find a purchaser. And everyone knew that the only possible purchaser was the United States Government.

CHAPTER XI
HOW PANAMA BECAME A REPUBLIC

"But I should wonder," said Goethe, as the great German poet was discussing with his friends, in 1827, the possibility of a Panama Canal, "if the United States were to let an opportunity escape of getting such a work into their own hands. It may be foreseen that this young state, with its decided predilection to the West, will, in thirty or forty years, have occupied and peopled the large tract of land beyond the Rocky Mountains. It may, furthermore, be foreseen that along the whole coast of the Pacific Ocean, where nature has already formed the most capacious and secure harbors, important commercial towns will gradually arise, for the furtherance of a great intercourse between China and the East Indies and the United States. In such a case it would be not only desirable but almost necessary that a more rapid communication should be maintained between the eastern and western shores of North America, both by merchant vessels and men-of-war, than has hitherto been possible with the tedious, disagreeable and expensive voyage round Cape Horn. I, therefore, repeat that it is absolutely indispensable for the United States to effect a passage from the Mexican Gulf to the Pacific Ocean, and I am certain that they will do it."

Less than twenty years after this prophecy, the United States, by the treaty of 1846, obtained from New Granada the perpetual right of transit for its citizens across the Isthmus of Panama, promising in return both to maintain the neutrality of any trade-routes that might be built there, and to guard the local government against attack by any foreign power. And ever since the making of this treaty and the building of the Panama Railroad, the Isthmus has been kept alive by American business and kept more or less peaceful by American ships and guns.

CHRISTENING THE FLAG OF THE REPUBLIC OF PANAMA AFTER THE REVOLUTION OF 1903.

Left to itself, the Isthmus would have been anything but peaceful. In the fifty-seven years between the treaty of 1846 and the final revolution in 1903, there were at least fifty-three disturbances and outbreaks, beginning with a riot in which two Americans were killed, and ending with a civil war nearly three years long. Six times our warships had to clear for action and land sailors and marines to protect life and property, and at four other times the government at Bogotá begged that United States troops be sent to Panama. This may surprise many people who believe that nothing of the kind ever happened in that country before 1903, but there were revolutions in Panama not only before then, and before 1846, but even before Nathaniel Bacon, our own first "revolutionist," rose against the royal governor of Virginia, and burned Jamestown in 1676. To understand this properly we must go back to the time of Balboa.

Balboa, Pizarro, Cortez, and all the other conquistadores, were men of the Middle Ages, living by the sword and despising honest labor. They were robber-barons, forcing the conquered Indians to pay them tribute in food and gold, and when there were no native warriors left to fight, they turned their swords against one another. And when, in 1543, the Emperor Charles V, urged by the good bishop Las Casas, decreed in his "New Laws for the Indies" that no more Indians must be enslaved or cruelly treated, Spain nearly lost America at that time, instead of two centuries and a half later. A fleet from Peru captured and plundered Old Panama, and, when reinforced and joined by the Panamanians, the Peruvians seized the whole Isthmus and held it in the name of Pizarro. Instead of an army, Charles V sent Pedro de la Gasca, a clever, smooth-tongued priest, who won back the leaders at Panama to allegiance to the emperor, and with their aid put down the rebellion in Peru. As Pedro de la Gasca was about to take ship for Spain at Nombre de Dios, after his triumphal return from Peru, the Contreras brothers, turbulent grandsons of old Pedrarias, came down the Pacific coast after raising a successful rebellion in Nicaragua, suddenly captured Old Panama and started to march across the Isthmus. But the citizens rose behind them, and the Contreras "revolution" came to a sudden and bloody end.

These old, half-forgotten fights among the early Spanish colonists in America were the children of all the feudal wars of Spain, and the fathers of all the nineteenth and twentieth-century revolutions of Spanish America. Fear of Drake and the bucaneers made the once-turbulent colonists glad to submit to the royal will for as much protection as the King could give them. He ruled like a feudal overlord,— a big bully over a crowd of little ones, — and when his power was ended, they all started up again. The Spanish Americans had nothing like the training in self-government and respect for law and order that our ancestors received both in England and here, for centuries before they won independence. The Spanish Americans have had to work it all out for themselves in the last hundred years or so, and a wonderfully good job they have made of it in that time; particularly in the big, stable republics of the south temperate zone. But in too many of the little countries along the shore of the Caribbean,—the region which a great American statesman has called "the land of the fantastic and the unexpected," men still prefer to vote as their forefathers did, with swords and cannon. Of all these backward countries, the one that has changed least since the days of the conquistadores is Colombia.

COLOMBIAN BARRACKS AND GARRISON IN
PANAMA CITY
Shortly before the revolution of 1903.

Panama was too small a state to stand alone, after it became independent of Spain, and accepted an invitation from Bogotá to put itself under the government there, but quickly found that it had exchanged King Log for King Stork. Almost immediately there were attempted revolts, and twice, in 1830 and again ten years later, the Isthmus won complete independence, and only returned to New Granada on promises of better treatment, solemnly made, but never realized. It was furthermore recognized, and set forth in the Constitution of that country, that Panama was a sovereign state, and that it or any one of the others had as much right to withdraw and set up an independent government as Virginia or New York or Massachusetts had under the old Articles of Confederation. But constitutions and written laws have never been worth much in those parts, except for musket-wadding. The local idea of government was to put yourself in power and then squeeze all the taxes you could out of everybody else. Nobody ever became president of New Granada or Colombia except by violence, and no president was strong enough to keep peace in Panama.

Revolutions, like every other industry, were revived on the Isthmus by the coming of the forty-niners and the building of the railroad. The Spaniards there have always been predatory by choice, and as they had lived off the Indians in the old days, they now lived off the Americans and other travelers. It is the old story of the robber-barons of a trade-route, fighting each other and their equally greedy overlord for the privilege of extorting toll from the traders passing through their territory. Panama in the nineteenth century was still in the Middle Ages. The landward walls of the city were torn down less than fifty years ago, and underground passages still connect the fortress-like, town houses of the *haciendados*, the rich landowners who used to make revolutions and fight them with armies of peons from their great estates, led by bands of foreign mercenaries or soldiers of fortune. These were the barons, and the overlord was the federal government at Bogotá, which exercised absentee tyranny of the worst kind.

As the Panamanians were not strong enough to win independence, nor the Bogotá government to keep good order, every revolution either degenerated into brigandage, or was stopped by American intervention. For the burden of this disorder fell not so heavily on the habitants of a region where there are no industries, and a poor man can gather a week's food in half an hour's walk through the jungle, as on the foreign merchants and traders, particularly the American-owned Panama Railroad. This company organized a police force of its own, called the Isthmus Guard, in 1855, and these fifty or so men, led by Ran Runnels, a Texas ranger, cleared the country of outlaws so thoroughly that in a few months they had abolished their own jobs. But only two years later, a dispute over the price of a slice of watermelon started a riot in which several American travelers were killed and hundreds of others, including many women, terrorized and plundered by the mob, the police and troops making no effort to stop the looting, but, instead, preventing the Americans from defending themselves.

Again and again our intervention was called for, and not always to defend our own people. Ferdinand de Lesseps brought fresh millions for the hungry, and his company was robbed by the local authorities almost as enthusiastically as by its own employees. During the scramble, revolutionists seized and burned Colon, with a great quantity of French canal stores. American marines were landed, restored order, and set the Colombian Humpty Dumpty up on his wall again. This was in 1885, and the successful general who made himself president that year proclaimed a new constitution which deprived Panama of all its rights as a sovereign state, and made it a mere province under the direct control of the federal government at Bogotá. Naturally there was great indignation on the Isthmus, and from then until the end there was an almost constant series of attempts to gain freedom.

The enforced dash of the battle-ship *Oregon* around South America in the Spanish-American War woke up the United States to its need of a quicker naval route between the two coasts. Congress authorized the purchase of the rights and property of the New French Canal Company for $40,000,000 an offer which that company was only too glad to accept, for, in 1903, its ten-year concession had nearly expired, and in another twelve months it might have no rights left to sell. We then offered the government of Colombia $10,000,000 for its permission to the Canal Company to make the sale, and for a new concession to the United States, allowing us to build and maintain the Canal.

The government of the so-called Republic of Colombia consisted, at this time, of one man, who had been elected vice-president but had kidnapped the president with a troop of cavalry and shut him up in an unsanitary dungeon, where he soon died. This interesting brigand had ruled ever since as president, without bothering about a congress, until he called one for the sole purpose of considering this offer of the United States. Hoping to get a higher price, and making no secret of their intention to wait until the French concession should run out and then demand some or all of the forty millions for themselves, the Colombian congress rejected our offer. They forgot what it meant to Panama.

Every inhabitant of the Isthmus knew that if the United States were not allowed to build the Canal there, it would build one across Nicaragua, where an American company already had a concession. If that were done, not only would Panama lose all its hoped-for prosperity, but even the railroad would cease to be operated, and the Isthmus would have as little trade or importance as in the eighteenth century. Naturally the Panamanians watched the Colombian congress anxiously, and, as soon as they saw the American treaty was doomed, began to prepare for a revolution.

CONCRETE BRIDGE ON ZONE HIGHWAY.

Everything was in their favor. The garrison had been left unpaid so long and had so many friends and sweethearts among the citizens that it was easily won over. Companies of men were organized, ostensibly as a fire-department, and rifles for them were smuggled in from New York. (There is as much romance and wickedness in the secret gun-trade of that city today as there ever was in bucaneering). Soon every prominent man on the Isthmus was in the plot, except the governor, who shut his eyes to it. Instead of the usual carpet-bagger from Bogotá, the newly appointed governor was Señor José Domingo de Obaldia, a man whose family have lived on the Isthmus for centuries, and he frankly told the Colombians that if the treaty were rejected, Panama would revolt, and he would do nothing to prevent it.

The treaty was rejected, and a date was at once set for the uprising. But the day before, a Colombian gunboat steamed into the harbor of

Colon, with four hundred and seventy-four conscripts and a few generals, who landed and demanded a train to take them to Panama City. The Bogotá government had at last become aware of the unsettled state of affairs on the Isthmus, which the American newspapers had been discussing openly for a month, and had sent this force to put an end to it—which it did, but not in the way they expected.

The Panama Railroad officials, whose sympathies were all with the revolutionists, sternly refused to let the army ride without paying cash fare. So the generals and their staff went on alone to Panama, to take command of the troops there. The revolutionists, warned by telegraph, hastened their preparations and when the generals entered the barrack square, the soldiers, instead of presenting arms, seized them and locked them up. At once the flag of the new Republic of Panama was run up over the city, and on two of the three gunboats in the harbor. The third fired a few shells, killing one Chinaman, and then sailed back to Colombia.

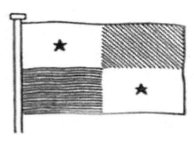

PANAMA
NATIONAL
FLAG.

Colonel Torres, who had been left in command of the Colombian troops at Colon, angrily declared that if the generals were not released and the new flags hauled down within an hour, he would kill every American in Colon. The women and children at once took refuge on two steamers, and the men gathered in the stone freight-house of the Panama Railroad, which had been strongly built for just such emergencies. But there was a small American gunboat, the *Nashville*, at Colon, and her captain landed forty-two sailors and marines. Torres then declared his great love for Americans, and a few days later he and his conscripts were bought up by the Panamanians for about twenty dollars apiece, and shipped back to where they came from.

QUARANTINE STATION ON CULEBRA ISLAND IN THE BAY OF PANAMA.

The Isthmus was now entirely in the hands of its own people, as it had been three times before; and three lines of action were open to the United States. The first was to intervene and force the Panamanians back under the rule of Bogotá, the second was to let the two sides fight it out to a finish. But we had tried both of these remedies again and again for over fifty years, and neither had availed to stop the endless bloodshed and destruction of property. The third course was to recognize the independence of the Republic of Panama, and forbid Colombia, now a foreign power, to land troops on the Isthmus. That was what President Roosevelt did, and the judgment of the American people was summed up in a remark made by a western congressman: "When that jack-rabbit jumped, I'm glad we did n't have a bow-legged man for President."

To any one acquainted with the history of the Isthmus, the Revolution of 1903, though almost equally sudden, appears no less natural than the jump of a startled jackrabbit; and indeed there was fifty times as much reason for it as for any of the fifty or more revolts that preceded it. Much as we wanted Panama, the Panamanians wanted us more, and if there was one thing experience had taught them it was how to organize a revolution. The charge that our government had "conspired" to bring it about was brought by persons utterly ignorant of the facts, flatly denied by President Roosevelt and his Secretary of State, Johy Hay; and the most rigid investigations by Congress have failed to reveal the slightest evidence either of the existence of such a conspiracy, or of the need of any external incentive for the Isthmus to revolt.

COAT OF ARMS OF THE REPUBLIC OF PANAMA.

The same orders were given the commanders of our war-ships as in several previous revolutions: to allow neither belligerent to land men or arms within fifty miles of either Panama or Colon. Colombia talked much of marching an army overland to the Isthmus, but that trail runs through the land of the San Blas Indians, and it would take a very strong army of white men to fight their way through that region, either then or today. Certain San Blas chiefs who had been made colonels in the Colombian army refused to fight the Panamanians; and the country of these Indians, though nominally in one or the other of the two republics, has been really an independent buffer state between them ever since 1903.

The Republic of Panama was quickly organized, with a constitution modeled on that of the United States, and a treaty was made between the two countries, by which the United States received the perpetual right to build and maintain a canal across the Isthmus, in return for the payment of $10,000,000. It also acquired possession of the Canal Zone, a strip of land five miles wide on either side of the Canal, and this bit of Central America is now as much United States territory as the parade ground at West Point. The two cities of Panama and Colon, however, were scalloped out of either end of the Zone and left part of the republic; but their ports, Balboa and Cristobal, became American, and the United States Government obtained the right to keep Panama and Colon clean, and to interfere whenever it thinks the native authorities cannot keep good order. For Uncle Sam was determined to make an end of filth and fever and petty warfare on the Isthmus, and get to work.

CHAPTER XII
HOW THE ISTHMUS WAS MADE HEALTHY

The New French Canal Company lost no time in accepting the $40,000,000, and its representative on the Isthmus formally turned over possession to the United States on May eighth, 1904. At this time, only about six hundred West Indians were working in the Cut, with a few side-excavators and trains of four-wheeled dump-cars, and an impatient call went up from the American people for their government to "make the dirt fly!" But for the next two and a half years, there was very little digging and a great deal of preparation.

Instead of hurrying thousands of laborers to the Isthmus to have them die there, as they did in the fifties and eighties, of fever and insufficient food, we cleaned house before we moved in. Clearings were made in the jungle, swamps were drained, old French houses were repaired and new ones were built. A line of steamers fitted with cold storage brought food from New York, and hotels or mess-houses served it to the men. The French hospitals at Ancon and Colon were enlarged, and the dirty little cities of Panama and Colon were cleaned and made sanitary. But though the filth was gone the fever remained.

In the same way, Havana and Santiago de Cuba, cities which old shipmasters declared they could smell ten miles to sea in an offshore breeze, had been thoroughly cleaned by our army as soon as the Spaniards evacuated Cuba in 1898, but still our soldiers had kept dying of yellow fever there. Everything that medical science could suggest was done to stop the spread of the disease, but without effect. Thousands sickened and hundreds died, while the doctors stood by, as one of them declared, "in utter perplexity and wonder."

SURGEON-GENERAL WILLIAM C. GORGAS.

No one knew how yellow fever was spread, though its ravages had been only too well known for two centuries and more. It had killed over thirty-six thousand people in Havana and a hundred and thirty thousand in Spain; it had swept our coast from Massachusetts to Florida, killing one person out of every ten in Philadelphia in 1793, and over

139

forty thousand in New Orleans between then and the end of the nineteenth century. Though other diseases, notably tuberculosis, have caused and still are causing much more direct suffering and loss of life, they were less feared because they lacked the terror of the unknown. When yellow fever broke out in a city, it was as if the very Angel of Death had come, walking invisible and slaying without cause. Then followed wild stampedes, brutally checked by "shotgun quarantines," looting, debauchery, and a wide-spread paralysis of business, causing altogether a loss of life and property impossible to compute.

Two things held yellow fever in check; frost stopped it, and those that recovered from the first attack were immune for the rest of their lives. Several regiments of these "immunes" were raised during the Spanish-American War, but there were not enough of them to garrison, all Cuba, and the disease soon broke out among the other troops sent there. Among non-immunes, and below the frost-line, what hope was there of stopping the spread of yellow fever? Only that some hero might strip this giant of his invisible coat, and, by showing what path he followed from death-bed to death-bed, enable us to guard and close it. That hero came, and in all our history there is no nobler story than that of his triumphant sacrifice.

It had long been suspected by several doctors that the germs of yellow fever were carried to fresh victims, neither by contact nor in infected clothing, but by certain species of mosquitos. Dr. Carlos

Finlay, an old Havana physician, had declared this belief as early as 1883. But no one could say for certain, because yellow fever is a disease that attacks only human beings, and to make the necessary experiments there were required, not mice or guinea-pigs, but living men.

One night in July, 1900, four surgeons of the United States Army Medical Corps met in Havana, where they had been sent as a Yellow-Fever Commission, and decided that the time had come when these experiments must be made. With full knowledge of the fearful nature of the disease, these doctors agreed that before they called for others to volunteer, they would make the first experiments on their own bodies.

But one of the four, Dr. Aristides Agramonte, a Cuban, was an immune and therefore could take no part in the tests; and another, Major Walter Reed, was almost immediately recalled to Washington. The two others, Jesse William Lazear, an American, and James Carroll, an Englishman, let themselves be bitten by mosquitos that had sucked the blood of yellow-fever patients. The experiment was but too successful. Both took the disease, Carroll recovered, but Lazear died. "Greater love hath no man than this, that a man lay down his life for his friends."

SANITARY SQUAD CLEANING PANAMA CITY.

A tablet, erected to the memory of Lazear, in Johns Hopkins Hospital at Baltimore, bears this inscription, written by President Eliot of Harvard University:

"With more than the courage and the devotion of the soldier, he risked and lost his life to show how a fearful pestilence is communicated and how its ravages may be prevented."

Volunteers were called for, that further experiments might be made, and General Leonard Wood, then military governor of Cuba, offered to pay each a reward of $200. When this was explained to the first men who came forward, two young soldiers from Ohio, John R. Kissinger and John J. Moran, both refused to accept it, declaring that they had volunteered "solely in the interest of humanity and the cause of science." Major Reed, to whom this declaration was made, rose to his feet, raised his hand to his forehead as if in the presence of his superior officer and said to these humble enlisted men, "Gentlemen, I salute you." When Major Reed told of this incident, not long afterwards, he declared, "In my opinion, this exhibition of moral courage has never been surpassed in the annals of the army of the United States."

Thanks to the skill of Major Reed, none of the thirteen men who followed the splendid example of Carroll and Lazear lost their lives; though some permitted themselves to be bitten by infected mosquitos and so took the fever, while their comrades entered a little room as dark and airless as the Black Hole of Calcutta, and slept there for three weeks, between blankets taken from the beds where yellow-fever patients had died. These last suffered nothing worse than discomfort, and it was conclusively proved that yellow fever is carried by the bite of a single species of mosquito; the *Stegomyia fasciata*, and by nothing else. This discovery, which has been truly said to be worth more than the entire cost of the Spanish War, gave the doctors something tangible to fight. Reed and Carroll drew up a complete program for protecting patients and killing off the mosquitos, and by putting it vigorously into effect, freed Cuba from yellow fever within a year.

Among Major Reed's assistants in Havana was Dr. William C. Gorgas, who was made chief sanitary officer of the Canal Zone shortly after the Americans came to Panama. Here he was confronted with a problem almost exactly like that which he had already seen solved in Cuba. All that was required was the intelligent and vigorous application of the principles discovered by the sacrifice of Lazear and elaborated by Carroll and Reed. Unfortunately, Dr. Gorgas was badly handicapped at the start by the failure of the United States Government to supply him with the force and funds necessary to do this.

The natural result was an outbreak of yellow fever, in Panama, in the spring and summer of 1905. Thirty-five of the American employees died, and hundreds more fled north as fast as they could find deck-room on the crowded ships. There they filled the newspapers with panic-stricken interviews and doleful prophecies that the Canal would never be built, and fervidly quoted this well-known stanza from the works of Gilbert, the poet of Colon.

> Beyond the Chagres River,
> 'T is said (the story's old)
> Are paths that lead to mountains
> Of purest virgin gold;
> But 't is my firm conviction,
> Whate'er the tales they tell,
> That beyond the Chagres River,
> All paths lead straight to Hell!

"There are three diseases in Panama," declared Mr. John L. Stevens, who became chief engineer at this time. "They are yellow fever, malaria, and cold feet; and the greatest of these is cold feet."

But now Dr. Gorgas was given his long-delayed medical supplies, his water-pipes, porch-screens, and plenty of money. Thousands of men were taken from the excavating force to swell the sanitary-squad. Best of all, the new governor of the Canal Zone—to whom the head of the Department of Sanitation was then subordinate—was Mr. Charles E. Magoon, who helped Dr. Gorgas with the greatest good-will and energy.

The first thing was to establish a rigid quarantine at both ports, to prevent new cases being brought in from other countries by sea. Every ship that came from a yellow-fever port was thoroughly fumigated to kill any infected mosquitos that might be on board, and all the passengers were kept in a screened house, where no local mosquitos could get at them, until long after the time required for the development and discovery of any possible fever-case among them. Without sick people to bite, the mosquitos could get no germs to carry, and, contrariwise, without the *Stegomyia* mosquito, the germs could not be carried from one person to another. Dr. Gorgas and his little army attacked the enemy from both directions at once.

The two great strongholds of the disease were the cities of Panama and Colon. Here the sanitary control which we had obtained by treaty-right was greatly helped by the fortunate fact that the first President of the Republic of Panama was Dr. Manuel Amador Guerrero, a well-trained physician and an authority on tropical diseases. At his suggestion, native doctors were appointed sanitary inspectors, and they did their work far more tactfully and with less friction than American inspectors could possibly have done, among a Spanish-speaking population, virtually all of whom were immune to yellow fever and had no idea of sanitation. They submitted with the greatest good-nature to having their houses entered and searched for yellow-fever patients, and during the worst of the epidemic, every house in Panama City was visited every day. As soon as a new case was discovered, the sick man was carried to the hospital in a screened ambulance, and his house and those of his neighbors were tightly sealed up with strips of paper and fumigated with sulphur, after which the dead mosquitoes were carefully swept up and burned. Then detective work would begin in two different directions: watching for new cases caused by mosquitos that might have bitten this man; and tracing back the source of his infection to some earlier and perhaps hitherto undiscovered case.

This would have been a well-nigh impossible task if the yellow-fever mosquito had been as strong on the wing as the more harmless species we know so well at home, most of whom can fly for miles with a favorable breeze. Fortunately, the *Stegomyia* is a feeble creature, usually living in or about houses, and rarely flying more than a hundred yards from its birthplace in some stagnant pool. The favorite breeding-places of these insects in Panama City were the rain-water barrels and cisterns, which were first screened and afterwards destroyed when the new waterworks were finished.

146

DR. JESSE W. LAZEAR, U.S.V.   DR. JOHN W. ROSS, U.S.A.   DR. JAMES CARROLL, U.S.V.
DR. CARLOS FINLAY.   MAJOR WALTER REED, U.S.A
JOHN R. KISSINGER.

The old waterworks consisted of two or three large Spanish wells, that received most of the drainage from the graveyard, and a few carts, from which the man who owned the graveyard used to peddle this water through the streets, for five cents a gallon. It was much better for his business than for the people who drank it. The Americans stopped this, and piped in good water from a reservoir made by damming the Rio Grande. There was a great celebration on the Fourth of July, 1905, when the water was turned on in the Cathedral Plaza. The

147

President, and the Governor, and all the other dignitaries, both Panamanian and American, attended a solemn high Mass in the cathedral, and at the elevation of the Host and the stroke of noon, the water was sent spurting into the air outside, and the Panamanian Republican Band struck up what it thought was the American national anthem. It was a popular tune of the period, called "Mr. Dooley"!

Sewers were laid at the same time as the water-pipes, and the big clumsy cobblestones were ground up in portable rock-crushers to make a concrete bed for the smooth new pavements of vitrified brick. Formerly, garbage of all sorts was thrown out into the streets to rot there or be eaten by the hundreds of vultures that were the only street-cleaning department. But now the streets are swept every night by gangs of negroes, employed by the Panamanian Government, under American supervision.

THE OLD WATER DEPARTMENT OF PANAMA.

In sanitation as in politics, we found Panama a city of the Middle Ages. Our doctors discovered a few wretched lunatics chained to the damp walls of the seventeenth-century dungeons, hewn out of the rock beneath the sea-wall; and lepers, who lived on the beach outside the city wall, and dared not come too near, lest people call out, "Unclean! Unclean!" and stone them, exactly as they did in Old Testament times. Though these unfortunates had no claim on our charity, our government at once built a modern insane asylum, first at Miraflores, and later at the Ancon hospital, and moved the lepers to a very beautiful little settlement called Palo Seco. There they are so well cared for that one man, whom our army doctors cured of a slight case of the disease, begged to be allowed to stay in that place for the rest of his life, and was made a hospital orderly there.

Driven out of the two cities, the harried *Stegomyia* found no refuge in the Canal Zone. There Dr. Gorgas's men cut down hundreds of acres of sheltering brush and high grass, dug miles of drainage ditches and covered all undrained pools and swamps with heavy oil that killed the mosquito larvae whenever they came to the surface to breathe. Holes were blown in old French dump-cars to keep them from holding water. To throw an empty tin can where it might become a breeding-place for mosquitoes was made a finable offense.

The epidemic of 1905 came to an end in September and the panic stopped with it. The last case of yellow fever on the Isthmus was in

November, 1906. Today, the *Stegomyia* mosquito is virtually extinct there, and so long as it is kept down and all foreign cases of the disease kept out, there will never be any more danger of an epidemic of yellow fever at Panama than at the North Pole. There is still a certain amount of "Chagres fever," which is nothing more or less than malaria. For the *Anopheles* mosquito, that carries the germ of this disease—a fact discovered by Dr. Ronald Ross of the British Army, in India in 1898—is a much stronger and hardier insect than the *Stegomyia*, and it is almost impossible to destroy it completely, especially round the smaller construction camps in the jungle. But there is much less malaria in Panama than in most parts of the United States.

One of the greatest and least-known triumphs of Dr. Gorgas and his organization was keeping the Isthmus free from the bubonic plague, at a time when this terrible disease, the "Black Death" that swept through Europe in the fourteenth century, was raging in the other Pacific ports both north and south of Panama. There it was confined to the three original cases brought in by sea, all of which proved fatal. This disease is carried, not by mosquitos, but by fleas, that travel on the backs of rats. A reward of ten cents was promptly offered for every rat tail brought in, and the rat is now a very scarce animal in Panama.

Dr. Gorgas was promoted to the rank of colonel in the United States Army Medical Corps, and made a member of the Isthmian Canal Commission in 1907. Though he has turned Panama from a pesthole into a health resort, there is still no lack of work there for him and for those who will come after him, for only by constant vigilance and costly sanitation can large bodies of Northern white men be kept healthy in the tropics. Moreover, if yellow fever or any other dangerous disease were ever again allowed to break out there, after Panama has become one of the great highways of the world, the Canal might easily prove as great a curse to humanity as it promises to be a blessing, for then ships would carry the sickness all too swiftly to all parts of the earth. Few physicians have ever had laid upon them a heavier burden or a more sacred trust than that of the chief sanitary officer of the Canal Zone, and all the world knows how well General Gorgas has discharged it. His name will go down in history as that of the man who freed the Isthmus from its most terrible enemy.

But General Gorgas would be the last man to deny that if it had not been for the work of his old chief and associates in Cuba in 1900-01, neither he nor any other man would have known how to fight yellow fever on the Isthmus in 1905. And if ever a fitting monument is raised, either in Panama or in the United States, to celebrate the building of the Canal and the victory of mankind over yellow fever, there should be graven high upon it the names of Reed and Carroll and Lazear.

CHAPTER XIII
HOW WE ARE BUILDING THE CANAL

To give a complete history of the building of the Canal, from the arrival of the first American steam-shovel to the final merging of the construction into the operating force, would take a library of little books like this. The best I can hope for is to give the reader some slight idea of what we might have seen, had we crossed the Isthmus together, in the days of the canal-builders. Let us imagine that we are taking such a trip.

As we steam into Limon Bay, after a two-thousand-mile voyage from New York, you will notice the long breakwater that is being built out from Toro Point, to make this a safe harbor, and also to keep storms and tides from washing the mud back into the four miles of canal that run under the sea to deep water. Down this channel comes something that looks like a very fat ocean steamer, and when it reaches the end it rises several feet in the water, turns round, and waddles back again. This is the sea-going dredge Caribbean, busy sucking up the bottom into its insides, and carrying it away. This craft is painted white, with a buff superstructure, as our warships used to be, and when it first came to the Isthmus, the quarantine officer put on his best suit of white duck, and went out to take breakfast on board the "battleship." Many other smaller dredges are dipping up rock into barges or pumping mud through long pipes to the land, all the way to the shore, and up the four miles of sea-level canal to where the Gatun Locks loom in the distance. All this you can see as we cross the bay to the ugly town of Colon, and its pretty suburb of Cristobal, which last is in the American Canal Zone, and the place where the steamers dock.

Now that you have seen what these dredges can do, you will ask me why we do not dig the rest of the Canal that way, instead of bothering with locks and dams, and I can give you the answer in five words: because of the Chagres River. This troublesome stream, as you can see by the map on page 4, comes down from the San Blas hills, strikes the line of the Canal at a place called "Bas Obispo," and zigzags across it to Gatun. And though we can dredge a channel up to Gatun, or scoop out the Gaillard Cut, which is an artificial cañon nine miles long through the hills between Bas Obispo and Pedro Miguel, on the Pacific side of the divide, we could not dig below the bed of the Chagres without having a lot of waterfalls pouring into the Canal, washing down the banks and silting up the channel. And as the Chagres is a sizable river that has been known to rise more than twenty-five feet in a night—for the rainfall at Panama is very severe—you can see that it is no easy problem to control it. But we have solved that problem by means of the Gatun Dam.

At Gatun, the valley of the Chagres is only about a mile and a quarter wide, and by closing the gap between the hills on either side with an artificial hill—for that is what the Gatun Dam really is—we accomplish two things: first, by backing up the river behind the dam, we form a deep lake that will float our ships up against the side of the hills at Bas Obispo, and make so much less digging in the Gaillard Cut; and, second, a flood that would cause a rise of twenty-five feet in the river would not cause one of a quarter of an inch in the big lake, that will have an area of nearly two hundred square miles.

In building the dam that is to hold back all this water, two trestles were driven across the valley, and from them were dumped many train-loads of hard rock from the Gaillard Cut, to form what the engineers call the "toes" of the dam. To fill the space between them, dredges pump in muddy water that filters away between the cracks of the toes, leaving the sediment it carried to settle and form a solid core of hard-packed clay, over a quarter of a mile thick. When the dam is finished, the side toward the lake will be thoroughly riprapped with stone to prevent washing by the waves, and so gentle will be the slope that you could ride over it on a bicycle without rising on the pedals.

To keep the water from running over the top of the dam, the engineers have cut a new channel for the Chagres through a natural hill of rock that stands in the center of the valley, and this, lined with concrete and fitted with regulating works, is what they call the "spillway." When the dam is finished, the spillway will be closed, and then the tremendously heavy rainfall—from ten to fifteen feet a year—will fill the lake in less than a twelvemonth. All the surplus water will run off through the spillway, and as it runs it will pass through turbines and turn dynamos to generate electricity for operating the machinery of the Gatun Locks that will lift ships over the dam.

FINISHED SECTION OF CULEBRA CUT AT BAS OBISPO.

The water in the drainage ditch is four feet below the level of the completed canal.

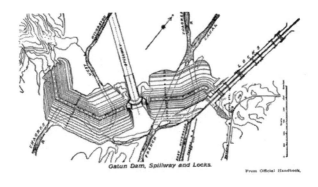

Gatun Dam, Spillway and Locks.

These locks are in pairs, like the two tracks of a railroad, so that ships can go up and down at the same time; three pairs, like a double stairway, of great concrete tanks each big enough for a ship a thousand feet long, a hundred and ten feet wide, and forty-two feet deep to float in it like a toy boat in a bath-tub. You can get some idea of their size when you remember that the *Titanic* was only eight hundred and fifty-two feet long. Or, to put it another way: every one of these six locks (and there are six more on the Pacific side) contains more concrete than there is stone in the biggest pyramid in Egypt. The American people have been able to do more in half a dozen years than the Pharaohs in a century, for our machinery has given us the power of many myriads of slaves.

And wonderful machinery it is at Gatun, both human and mechanical. It is not easy for a visitor, standing on one of the lock walls—which, as you can see from the diagram, is as high as a six-story house—and looking clown into the swarming, clanging lock-pits, to see any system, but if he look

156

closely, he can trace its main outlines. Up the straight four-mile channel from Limon Bay come many barges, towed either by sturdy sea-going tugs or an outlandish-looking, stern-wheel steamer called the *Exotic*. Some of these barges are laden with Portland cement from the United States, others with sand from the beaches of Nombre de Dios, or crushed stone from the quarries of Porto Bello. (For both of these old Spanish ports are now alive again, helping in the building of the Canal, and every now and then one of our dredges strikes the hull of a sunken galleon, or brings up cannon-balls or pieces-of-eight.) The cargoes of all these barges are snatched up by giant unloader-cranes and put into storehouses, out of which, like chicks from a brooder, run intelligent little electric cars that need no motormen, but climb of themselves up into the top story of the dusty mixing-house. Here, eight huge rotary mixers churn the three elements, cement, sand, and stone, into concrete, and drop it wetly into great skips or buckets, two of which sit on each car of a somewhat larger-sized system of electric trains, whose tracks run along one side of the lock-pits. Presently those skips rise in the air and go sailing across the lock-pit in the grip of a carrier traveling on a steel cable stretched between two of the tall skeleton towers that stand on either side of the lock-site. When the skip is squarely above the one of the high steel molds it is to help fill, it is tilted up, and there is so much more concrete in place.

GATUN LOCKS
Steel frame for casting a section of the square centre wall.

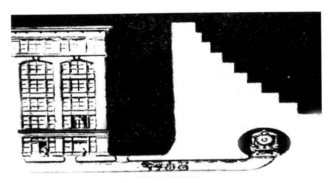

SECTIONAL VIEW OF A LOCK, AS HIGH AS A SIX-STORY BUILDING.

The tube through which the water Is admitted is large enough to hold a locomotive.

When the last cubic yard has been set, the gates hung, and the water turned in, a ship coming from the Atlantic will stop in the forebay or vestibule of the lowest right-hand locks, and make fast to electric towing-locomotives running along the top of the lock-walls. No vessel will be allowed to enter a lock under her own power, for fear of her ramming a gate and letting the water out, as a steamer did a few years ago in the "Soo" Locks, between Lake Huron and Lake Superior. Every possible precaution has been taken to prevent such an accident at Gatun. Any ship that tried to steam into one of the locks there, for any reason whatsoever, would first have to carry away a heavy steel chain, that will always be raised from the bottom as a vessel approaches, and never lowered until she has come to a full stop. Then the runaway ship would crash, not into the gates that hold back the water, but a pair of massive "Guard gates," placed below the others for this very purpose.

PEDRO MIGUEL LOCKS
Arches for carrying the touring locomotive tracks from level to level.

"The lock gates will be steel structures seven feet thick, sixty-five feet long, and from forty-seven to eighty-two high. They will weigh from three

159

hundred to six hundred tons each. Ninety-two leaves will be required for the entire Canal, the total weighing fifty-seven thousand tons. Intermediate gates will be used in the locks, in order to save water and time, if desired, in locking small vessels through, the gates being so placed as to divide the locks into chambers six hundred and four hundred feet long, respectively. Ninety-five per cent, of the vessels navigating the high seas are less than six hundred feet long."

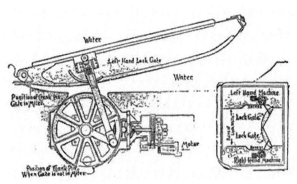

A BIRD'S-EYE VIEW OF ONE OF THE NINETY-TWO PANAMA
"BULL-WHEELS."
This wheel was invented by Mr. Edward Schildhauer of the Isthmian Canal Commission. The wheel revolves horizontally and thrusts out from the side of each lock-wall a long steel arm that opens and closes one of the huge lock-gates. These gates are of the "miter" pattern, so called because, when closed, they make a blunt wedge pointing up-stream, like the slope of a bishop's miter. Observe the curved and hollowed recesses in the lock-walls into which the open gates fold back, like the blades of a knife into the handle. There are, of course, two "bull-wheels"; one for each of the gates.

160

You will notice that each leaf of a pair of these gates is sixty-five feet long, instead of fifty-five or half the width of a lock. When they are closed, they form a blunt wedge pointing upstream, and the pressure of the water only keeps them tighter shut. Finally, if all the gates were swept away, there would still remain the "emergency dam" at the head of each flight of locks, ready to be swung round and dropped into position like a portcullis.

From Official Handbook.

CROSS SECTION OF LOCK CHAMBER AND WALLS OF LOCKS.

A—Passageway for operators.
B—Gallery for electric wires.
C—Drainage gallery.
D—Culvert in center wall.
E—Culverts under the lock floor.
F—Wells opening from lateral culverts into lock chamber.
G—Culvert in sidewalls.
H—Lateral culverts.

From Official Handbook.

CROSS SECTION OF LOCK CHAMBER AND WALLS OF LOCKS.

A—Passageway for operators.

B—Gallery for electric wires.

C—Drainage gallery.

D—Culvert in center wall.

E—Culverts under the lock floor.

F—Wells opening from lateral culverts into lock chamber.

G—Culvert in sidewalls.

H—Lateral culverts.

161

Once a ship is inside, the lower gates will be closed behind her by machinery hidden in the square center-pier, valves will be opened, and water from the lake will rush down the conduits in the walls and flow quietly in from below, until it has reached the level of the lock above. Then the upper gates will open, and the electric locomotives,—there will be four of them to handle every big ship, one at each corner,—will go clicking and scrambling up the cog-tracks carried on broad, graceful arches from level to level, and then pull the ship through after them. In like manner will she pass through the two upper locks, and out on the wide waters of Gatun Lake, eighty-five feet above the level of the sea.

The average time of filling and emptying a lock will be about fifteen minutes, without opening the valves so suddenly as to create disturbing currents in the locks or approaches. The time required to pass a vessel through all the locks is estimated at three hours; one hour and a half in the three locks at Gatun, and about the same time in the three locks on the Pacific side. The time of passage of a vessel through the entire canal (about fifty miles from deep water in one ocean to deep water in the other; forty from beach to beach), is estimated as ranging from ten to twelve hours, according to the size of the ship, and the rate of speed at which it can travel."

The time spent by a ship in the locks at Panama will be more than made up by the much greater ease and speed with which she will be able to navigate the rest of the Canal there, as compared with that at Suez, where steamers must crawl at a snail's pace, or the wash from their propellors will bring down the sandy banks; and two large liners cannot meet and pass without one of them having to stop and tie up to the shore. At no place on the Panama Canal will this be necessary, for even at its narrowest part—the nine miles through the Gaillard Cut—the channel will be three hundred feet wide at the bottom, giving plenty of elbow-room for the largest ships, and lined with concrete where it is not hewn out of solid rock. The under-water and sea-level sections at either entrance will be five hundred feet wide, and through the greater part of the Gatun Lake, a ship will steam at full speed down a magnificent channel one thousand feet broad, with no more danger of washing the banks than if she were in the middle of the lower Amazon.

To help night navigation, there will be long rows of acetylene buoys, so ingeniously made that the difference of a few degrees of heat regularly caused on the Isthmus by the rising and setting of the sun, will serve to turn their light off and on, by expanding and contracting a little copper rod. This device, invented by one of the American canal employees, has been thoroughly tested, and found to work perfectly. Everywhere trim little concrete lighthouses, looking strange enough in the jungle, are being built, or, rather, cast in one piece, on wooded hilltops that will soon be islands.

Already the yellow water is rapidly backing up, as the dam and the spillway gates are being raised.

You can mark the spread of the lake by the gray of the dying, drowned-out trees against the green of the living jungle. Only in the channel and the anchorage basin has Gatun Lake been cleared of timber, and the greater part of it will be a mass of stumps and snags. The centuries-old trade-route down the Chagres has been wiped out, and more than a dozen little towns and villages, Ahorca Lagarto, Frijoles, San Pablo, Matachin, have been moved to new sites on higher ground. It was not easy to make the natives believe that these places that had been inhabited for hundreds of years would soon be under forty feet of water. Some thought the Americans were prophesying a second deluge. "Ah, no, Señores," protested one old Spaniard, "the good God destroyed the world that way once, but He will never do so again."

RELOCATING THE PANAMA RAILROAD

The Panama Railroad, too, has been relocated for its entire length, except for two miles or so out of Panama City, and a little over four miles between Colon and Gatun. Both the former station and the old village at Gatun (which is the place where Morgan's bucaneers and the Forty-niners, and all the other travelers up-river spent the first night) are now buried under the huge mass of the Gatun Dam, The former line of the Panama Railroad through the lake-bed, though double-tracked and modernized only a few years ago, has been completely abandoned. The new, permanent, single-track road swings to the east at Gatun, and runs on high ground round the shore of the lake to a bridge across the Chagres at Gamboa, a little above Bas Obispo. It was originally planned that the railroad should run from here through the Gaillard Cut on a "berm" or shelf, ten feet above the surface of the water, but the many slides caused this to be abandoned, and the line was built through the hills on the eastern side of the Cut. At Miraflores it runs through the only tunnel on the Isthmus. Because of the very heavy cuts and fills, the relocation of the Panama Railroad has cost $9,000,000, or $1,000,000 more than building the original road, although the new line is about a mile shorter. It is very solidly built, with steel bridges, concrete culverts, steel telegraph poles, made of lengths of old French rails bolted together and set up on end, and embankments filled with several million cubic yards of rock from the Cut.

Only a little rock was taken out of the Gaillard Cut by the French, most of their digging being what the engineers call "soft-ground work." But the deeper part of the great nine-mile trench, which they left for the Americans to dig, is almost entirely a "hard-rock job." From Bas Obispo to Pedro Miguel (which every American on the Isthmus calls "Peter Magill") it must be hewn and blasted out of solid stone. Row above row of steam or compressed-air drills are boring deep holes in the terraces beneath them, and gangs of men are kept busy filling these holes with dynamite. As much as twenty-six tons were used in one blast, when an entire hillside was blown to pieces, and twice every day, when the men have left the Cut for lunch or to go home, hundreds of reports go rattling off like a bombardment.

Then they move up the great steam-shovels to dig out the shattered rock with their sharp-toothed steel "dippers" that can pick up five cubic yards or eight tons, at a time. Think how bulky a ton of coal looks in the cellar, and then imagine eight times that much being lifted in the air, swung across a railroad track, and dropped on a flat-car, as easily as a grocer's clerk would scoop up a pound of sugar and pour it into a paper bag. Boulders too large to handle conveniently are broken up with "dobey shots," small charges of dynamite stuck into crevices, and tamped down with adobe clay. So skilful are the steam-shovel men (all Americans), that they will make one of their huge machines pick up a little pebble rolling down the side of the Cut as easily as you could with your hand; and every one of them is racing the others, and trying to beat the last man's record for a day's excavation. The present record was made on March twenty-second, 1910, when four thousand, eight hundred and twenty-three cubic yards of rock, or eight thousand, three hundred and ninety-five tons were excavated in eight hours by one machine. There are one hundred of these steam-shovels on the Isthmus, and more than fifty of them in the Gaillard Cut, and to see them all purring and rooting together, more like a herd of living monsters than a collection of machinery, is one of the most wonderful spectacles in the world.

Sometimes steam-shovels will be caught and buried by a "slide," an avalanche of rock or a river of mud brought down by some weakness in the banks. Wrecking trains and powerful railroad-cranes are always kept ready to go to their rescue. The worst place is across the Cut from the town of Culebra, where forty-seven acres of hillside are crawling down like a glacier. This is the famous Cucaracha Slide, that began to trouble the French as long ago as 1884; and though two million cubic yards of it have been dug away, there is half as much more to come. Altogether, this slide and the twenty others will have brought twenty million cubic yards of extra material to be taken out of the Cut, by the time the Canal is finished. But our engineers have learned how to stop them, by cutting away the weight at the top of each slide, and that, and the pressure of the water in the finished canal, should keep the banks at rest.

To carry away the rock and earth dug out by the steam-shovels, there is an elaborate railroad system of several hundred miles of track, so ingeniously arranged that the loaded trains travel down-grade and only empty cars have to be hauled up hill. Much rock is used on the Gatun Dam, and also on the breakwaters at either end of the Canal, but most of the material excavated from the Cut is disposed of by filling up swamps and valleys. Every dirt-train (they would call it that on the Isthmus even if it carried nothing but lumps of rock as big as grand pianos), travels an average distance of ten miles to the dumps and has the right of way over passenger trains, specials, and even mail trains. Only for the President of the United States has the line ever been cleared.

At the dumping-ground, each dirt-train is run out on a trestle, and unloaded in one of two ways. If it is composed of steel dump-cars, they are tipped up either by hand or compressed air. Most of the trains, however, are of big wooden flat-cars, raised on one side, and connected by steel flaps or "aprons," so that a heavy steel wedge, like a snow-plow, can be drawn from one end of the train to the other by a windlass and cable, thus clearing all the cars in a jiffy. (It is great fun to ride on the big wedge when they are "plowing-off.") When the dirt begins to rise above the edge of the trestle, a locomotive pushes up a machine called the "spreader," that smooths it out into a level embankment, and then another machine, the "track-shifter," picks up the ties and rails bodily, and swings them over to the edge of the new ground. Each of these machines does the work of hundreds of laborers.

LIDGERWOOD FLATS BEING UNLOADED
Balboa Dumps, low tide, March, 1908.

A SPREADER

Balboa Dumps, low tide, March, 1908.

Two large machine shops, now at Gorgona and Empire, but soon to be moved to Balboa, at the Pacific end of the Canal, are kept busy assembling new machinery brought down from the United States, and repairing the worn parts of the steam-shovels, the hundreds of locomotives and thousands of cars. At Mount Hope, near Colon, is a shipyard for the tugs and dredges of the Atlantic division, and a huge general storage yard and warehouse for everything from a ten-ton casting for a lock-gate to a box of thumb-tacks for fastening a blueprint of that gate to a drawing-board. Every necessary article is there and in its proper place; and the same is true of the tool-box of the smallest switch-engine. From the top to the bottom there is neither skimping nor waste, but an efficiency like that of a Japanese army in the field.

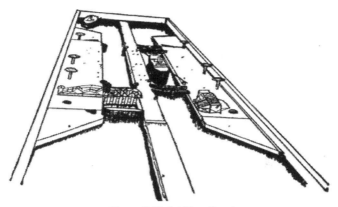

From Official Handbook.
MODEL OF PEDRO MIGUEL LOCKS.

At Pedro Miguel a ship from the Atlantic will begin the descent on the other side of the divide. The locks on the Pacific side are exactly like those at Gatun, except that instead of having all three pairs together, there is one pair here and two at Miraflores, with a little lake between. From Miraflores, the Canal is being dredged out at sea-level to its Pacific terminus at Balboa, where there will be great docks and warehouses and shipyards on land that has been made by filling in tidal marshes with dirt from the Gaillard Cut. As on the Atlantic side, the Canal will run four miles out under the sea to deep water; and to protect it from storms, a breakwater is being built from the shore to Naos Island, in the Bay of Panama. It is both

171

strange and appropriate that the Panama Canal should have one of its entrances at this island, whose name, the Spanish word for "ship," reminds us that three hundred and fifty years ago it was the port of the city of Old Panama.

CHAPTER XIV
HOW WE LIVE ON THE ISTHMUS TODAY

When Bill Smith, steam-shovelman, went to Panama in 1904, he wrote to his wife in Kansas City that it looked to him like a pretty tough camp. The food was bad and the water was worse, and there wasn't enough of either. His quarters were in an old French house full of scorpions, and the only mirror he could find to shave himself in was a broken piece of window-glass tilted back against the wall. Some of the boys were living in tents, and others in native shacks with mud floors, thatched roofs full of snakes, and walls you could throw a cat through. There was no place for a man to go after he finished his day's work but a saloon full of bad liquor or a crooked gambling-house. Two of the men who came down with him had died of fever, and three more had gone back on the next boat north. But Bill Smith thought he would stick it out a little longer. It took more than a little courage to make that resolution in 1904.

In 1912, Bill is still on the Isthmus, and Mrs. Smith and the children are there too. They are living rent-free in a "Type 17 House," a neat little cottage that Uncle Sam has not only built for them, but also furnished, from the concrete piles it stands on, to the ventilator in the galvanized-iron roof. Grass rugs, mission furniture, silverware, bed linen, coal for the kitchen range, all are provided by the

United States Government, to say nothing of free electric light, and a free government telephone. The wide veranda is screened with copper netting (iron would rust too quickly) to keep out the few mosquitos that have escaped Colonel Gorgas. The garden is planted with flowers provided by the quartermaster's department, and a cement walk leads to the macadamized and electric-lighted street that eight years ago was covered with primeval jungle.

They dine well at the Smiths', though virtually every mouthful of their food has to be brought by sea from New York or New Orleans, in ships fitted with cold-storage. From the great storehouse at Mount Hope, every morning a long train of refrigerator-cars crosses the Isthmus, and brings fresh supplies to the hotels and local commissaries in all the camps and towns. A bachelor, quartered in a hotel, comes down from his comfortably furnished room that costs him nothing, to a meal that costs him thirty cents, and which he would be lucky to get in New York for less than a dollar. Mrs. Smith buys her meat and groceries at the commissary store at wholesale prices. But in neither case is anything sold for money. Everything is paid for with checks torn out of booklets issued to employees and charged against their salaries, and with these you can buy anything from a pair of khaki trousers to an ice-cream soda. For Uncle Sam began by supplying frontier necessities, and ended by providing every luxury that you would expect to find in a thriving community of ten thousand Americans.

STREET OF MARRIED QUARTERS AT PEDRO MIGUEL.

TYPICAL DINING ROOM IN ISTHMIAN CANAL COMMISSION HOTEL.

The life of the five thousand American engineers and clerks and foremen, and that of their wives and children, is very much like what it would be at home. Though it is summer all the year round, the temperature seldom rises above eighty-six, and it is always cool and pleasant at night. There are band concerts, and firemen's tournaments,—there is a well-equipped and efficient fire department,—and women's clubs, and church societies, and a Panama Canal baseball league.

Hundreds of sturdy, sunburned American children (for though the English cannot raise healthy white children in India, we can in Panama) go galloping about on little native ponies, or study in the Canal Zone public schools. The pupils of the high school publish a monthly paper called the *Zonian*. Several patrols of boy-scouts have been organized, and they have the advantage of a real jungle to scout in.

Uncle Sam had no intention of becoming a benevolent landlord and caterer when he went to Panama to dig the Canal. But in order to get the best class of American workingmen, and keep them fit to do their best work, he had to keep adding one thing after another, until now there are government laundries, bakeries with automatic pie, cake, and breadmaking machines, electric-light plants, ice factories, plants for roasting coffee and freezing ice cream; a harness shop, livery stables, printing-press, and an official newspaper, the *Canal Record*.

If Bill Smith were struck by a flying fragment of rock after a too-heavy blast in the Cut, he would find a first-aid package beside his seat on the steam-shovel, receive free treatment at Ancon or Colon Hospital, and spend his convalescence at the comfortable rest-home on the beautiful island of Taboga in Panama Bay. Instead of losing his pay in gambling, which is strictly forbidden and effectively kept out of the Zone, he and the other employees send home over a quarter of a million dollars worth of postal money-orders every month. He no longer spends his noon hours and evenings at a saloon, but at one of the Government club-houses or recreation-buildings, reading, bowling, playing basket-ball, and otherwise enjoying himself. Or he can drop into the lodge-room of his fraternal order,—as an "old Canal man" of 1904, Bill Smith would certainly belong either to the "Incas," or the "Society of the Chagres." He works for union hours for better than union pay, and every year he and his family are given first-class passages at reduced rates to New York and back on one of the Government-owned ships of the Panama Railroad Steamship Line, and a six-weeks' vacation in the United States.

Bill Smith is not a real man, but his name is the only thing about him that is "make-believe." He is a typical example of the employees on the "gold roll," virtually all of whom are American citizens. But even with such housing and treatment and an annual trip to colder and more bracing air, a northern white man could not do good pick-and-shovel work in the tropics. So the great bulk of the force, below the grade of foreman, is drawn from

177

the warmer parts of the world. Because they were at first paid in Panamanian silver, whose face value is worth only half that of American gold, they are known as the "silver roll men."

Of the thirty thousand and more common laborers, the great majority are negroes from Jamaica or Barbados, or other parts of the British West Indies. They are very peaceable and law-abiding fellows, but exceedingly lazy, and unbelievably stupid. There is room in their heads for exactly one idea at a time, and no more. One of them was given a red flag by the foreman of a section-gang on the Panama Railroad, and told to go round the curve and stop any train that might come along, while they replaced a rail. He went to his post, and just as they had taken up the rail, a switch-engine came sailing round the corner, flew off the track, and nearly killed two men. When they asked the Jamaican why he had failed to flag it, he replied, "You told me to stop *trains*. That wasn't a train, it was a locomotive."

When the Irish-American foreman started to say what he thought of him, the Jamaican ran away to the British consul, and complained that he was being called names. These big, strong, black men have to be looked after like so many children. Before we stopped them, they used to sleep in their rain-soaked clothes, waste their lunch-money on perfumery or lottery-tickets, and come to their work half-starved and sickly. Now they get three good hot meals a day, besides better pay and quarters than they ever dreamed of in Jamaica. Besides, they have learned that if they do not work, we can get other men to fill their places.

SHIFTING TRACK BY HAND.

TRACK SHIFTING MACHINE.

To stimulate the Jamaicans by competition, we have brought over several thousand peasants from Galicia, in the north of Spain, and these men, being strong and healthy and used to labor in a hot climate for a fraction of what they earn on the Isthmus, do very good work. Each of them gets twice as much as a Jamaican, and more than earns it. Many of the Gallegos stick to their picturesque flat velvet caps and gay sashes. Then there are Italians, and Greeks, and Armenians, and Turks, and French-speaking negroes from Martinique, and turbaned coolies from India, and ever so many more besides. There are no Chinese or Japanese coolies, because the Republic of Panama excludes them by law, as does the United States. But almost everywhere in the two cities and the Zone, you can find a prosperous Chinese storekeeper, who was a coolie in the days of de Lesseps.

It is a motley and interesting crowd that throngs round the pay-car when it goes over the line twice a month. At every stop the men file up steps on one side of the car and down the other, past open counters piled high with silver and gold. (Several times the springs of the pay-car have been broken by the weight of its load of coin.) The men are paid, not by name, because most of them cannot write, and many of them often change their names whenever a new one strikes their fancy, but by the number on the brass check which every employee carries at his belt. There has never been any attempt to "hold up" the pay-train, though it is only guarded by half a dozen policemen. But they are very bad men to start a fight with, these tall, bronzed ex-troopers of the United States Cavalry, in the smart olive-green uniform of the Zone Police. They are the men who have made brigandage a lost art on the Isthmus, and taught the Panamanians to vote with ballots instead of machetes and Mauser rifles. About two hundred and fifty of this efficient little military constabulary, much resembling the Canadian Northwest Mounted Police, keep the four hundred square miles of the Canal Zone as peaceful as a New England village on Sunday morning. All the officers and first-class troopers of this force are Americans, and about seventy-five second-class troopers are Jamaican negroes, who have served in the British West Indian Constabulary, or the British West Indian Regiment. These are very fine, soldierly men, far more intelligent than the average Jamaican. They are used to police their own countrymen on the Isthmus, which they do with much more tact and less friction than an American could.

Anyone who mistakes the Canal Zone of today for a lawless frontier community is more than likely to find himself making roads with the rest of the chain-gang. There are three United States Circuit Courts on the Isthmus, and the three justices sit together as the Supreme Court of the Canal Zone. As a rule, they sit without a jury, for most of the laborers come from countries where jury trials are unknown. Interpreters skilled in many tongues are as much needed as in the police courts of New

York. A code of laws has been put in force, to take the place of the clumsy and cruel old Spanish laws we found when we came to the Isthmus. A penitentiary at Culebra contains such prisoners as are not working on the roads. If a convict breaks jail, there is no place for him to run to, for on each side of the Canal Zone stretches almost unbroken jungle, and there is a Zone policeman standing at the gangway of every steamer.

SEAL OF THE CANAL ZONE.
From Official Handbook.

Roads were an unknown luxury on the Isthmus in 1904, except for the muddy streets of the towns and a few rough trails through the jungle. Now there are many miles of macadamized highway, with concrete drains and bridges, and some day these will be connected to form an automobile speedway from ocean to ocean. One of the first-built and best-known bits of road is the three-mile drive from Panama City out over the beautiful rolling plain of Las Sabanas, to where the red-roofed *haciendas*, or summer bungalows, of the native aristocracy stand under the palm-trees. Here the rich citizens of Panama City spend the dry season, in primitive shacks, all doors and no windows, that an American dry-goods clerk would turn up his nose at for a week-end camp. But even the poorest of them has plenty of grounds round it and a more or less elaborate gateway, and if you do not go near enough to notice the sickly chickens peeking round the touring-car in the drive, and the fat women in loose wrappers shading themselves on the veranda, the effect is not so bad.

When I was writing this book at my father's house in Ancon, in the dry season of 1912, we used frequently to take a gallop on Las Sabanas in the afternoons. Very varied and interesting were the people we met on the road: pretty American trained-nurses riding astride, and rice-powdered señoritas leaning back in victorias; a farmer from the hills, with rude sandals on his feet and a three-foot machete thrust through his red sash, driving three tiny donkeys laden with yams and cocoanuts; a string of motor-cars full of American tourists, bound for the ruins of Old Panama (they'll be going there in trolley-cars before the Canal is opened); a big Zone Police trooper saluting the President of Panama in his heavy carriage, painted with the arms of the republic; and two black-robed priests talking to a sturdy negro boy, whose only covering was the water running down his back from the five-gallon Standard Oil tin he was carrying on his shoulder, by way of a bucket. Often, when we cantered home through the swarming negro suburb of Calidonia, and up over the high-arched bridge across the tracks at the Panama Railroad station, I thought how for a hundred yards that road had been covered with dead and dying men, when a charging column of revolutionists was raked by a machine-gun placed on that bridge and operated by an American soldier of fortune in the Colombian service. That was in the unsuccessful revolution of 1901. Today that soldier of fortune is a drill-foreman in the Cut.

At the Panama Railroad station (they are building a handsome new one of terra-cotta and concrete), you can take a "spickety" cab to any part of Panama City, or the American suburb of Ancon for ten cents, American, or twenty cents, spickety. What is "spickety"? When the Americans first came to the Isthmus, the drivers of the native cabs (rickety little two-seated buggies drawn by ponies as big as rabbits) used to cry, "Me speak it, the English!" which meant "I speak English," but sounded like "Me spickety English." So our men began to call their speech "spickety English," and their cabs "spickety cabs," and now everything Panamanian is spickety.

On the side of Ancon Hill, a small volcano, extinct since prehistoric times, between the port of Balboa and the city of Panama, is the American settlement of Ancon. It is a very beautiful town, that has no named or numbered streets, but is like a garden laid out in terraces with pretty little houses here and there, and a big red-tiled administration building for the Governor, and the Canal Commissioners. Here, too, is the Ancon Hospital, built by the French, and a large hotel, called the Tivoli, that is run by the United States Government through the War Department. It was built as a social center for the Americans on the canal force, and they are changed two-thirds as much as the tourists that stop there. The Tivoli would be considered a very good summer hotel anywhere in the United States, and if you want to engage a room there during the dry season, when the flood of visitors is at its height, you had better cable in advance.

Two white posts on either side of the road from the Tivoli to the railroad station mark the Zone line, and the place where a President of the United States first entered foreign territory. That was in 1906, when Theodore Roosevelt drove down the Avenida Central, and made a speech from the steps of the cathedral.

The Avenida Central or Central Avenue—a hundred years ago they called it the Calle Real or the Royal Road—is the great thoroughfare of Panama City. It runs from the railroad station to the Cathedral Plaza. For the first mile or so it passes through the tawdry new quarter that has shot up like a Western boom-town since 1904, round what used to be the little suburb of Santa Anna, outside the city wall. The old church of Santa Anna—once the family chapel of a Spanish grandee—still stands on the plaza of that name, with a dance-hall on one side, a vaudeville theater on the other, and saloons all round it.

A SQUAD OF MOUNTED ZONE-POLICE IN THE
FRONT OF THE ANCON HOSPITAL.

A few blocks beyond Santa Anna Plaza, you pass a street-shrine with ever-lighted candles that marks the site of the landward gate, and enter the old part of the town. Here the houses have walls three feet thick, and narrow windows with very stout shutters, for, in the disorderly old days, it was frequently necessary to turn them into fortresses on short notice. Even the churches were loopholed for musketry, and they are still connected by underground passages with the cathedral in the center of the town. When you walk down one of the narrow streets at night, under the long double row of Spanish balconies, you half expect to see a file of halberdiers go clanking past in the moonlight, or to hear the "clink and fall of swords." But all you hear is a cheap phonograph playing an American popular song of the year before last, and the only armed men you meet are self-important little native policemen, about four and a half feet high. It takes several of them to arrest one drunken Canal laborer.

This national police is the nearest approach to an army they have in Panama. On the site of the old Colombian barracks, the Panamanians have built a handsome Government Palace, that is a combination White House, Treasury Building, and National Theater. Whenever the President wishes to go to the theater, all he has to do is to walk down a short corridor running directly from his apartments to his official box.

Over on the other side of the city, just across the street from Ancon, stands the new National Institute, that is to be the university and normal school of Panama. At present, its pupils have not advanced beyond the primary grades, which speaks eloquently of the lack of public education under the old régime, and the determination of the Panamanians that their children shall not grow up in ignorance.

Some of the other "improvements" the Panamanians have made are, unfortunately, in much worse taste. They have painted the time-mellowed cathedral and most of the churches—the oldest of which was built in 1688—until they look like brand-new suburban villas; they have clapped a tin roof over the moss-grown tiles of the lovely little chapel on Taboga Island, turned the ruined Jesuit monastery into an apartment-house, and are now proposing to tear down what is left of the Church of San Domingo, with its famous earthquake-defying "flat arch," that "is the wonder

187

of every visiting engineer and architect. Even if they care nothing for the monuments of their own past, any European hotel-keeper could tell the Panamanians that they would make more money by exhibiting their ruins to American tourists than by tearing them down.

Almost everybody you meet on the streets of Panama wears American ready-made clothing, and there is almost nothing in the stores but cheap American goods. Every year a few ship loads of German-made curios and imitation Panama hats are imported to sell to the tourists. The finest and softest of the so-called "Panama" hats—the kind you can fold up and put in an envelope without cracking them—are made in Ecuador, and a coarser sort in Peru. No Panama hats are made in Panama. In fact, there are no manufactures there of any sort, and therefore, as everything must be imported, there is only a low tariff. As a result, you can sometimes buy Chinese silks or European novelties for less than you would pay in the United States, and there are one or two little shops where genuine Ecuador hats are sold for a quarter of what they would bring in New York. Or, if you are very lucky, you may be able to pick up a necklace of old Spanish goldsmith's work, but there are not many of those left. Most of the things that are shown you on the Isthmus as "old Spanish" are about as genuine as the "old Spanish gun" on that part of the sea-wall called Las Bovedas, not far from where the fishermen beach their boats at low tide, and the townspeople walk out and hold a market on the sea-bottom. This cannon—which they will tell you was used against the bucaneers—is a Parrott rifle of the type used in our Civil War, and has stamped on one of its trunnions the date "1864."

From the founding of the city to the present day, the heart and soul of Panama has been the Cathedral Plaza. Here the Isthmus declared its independence from Spain, and, later, from Colombia. After the latter event, an attempt was made to change the name of the square to "Independence Plaza," but the new name has failed to stick. The cathedral was built about the middle of the eighteenth century by a negro, who, though born the son of a poor charcoal burner, was the first of his race to become the bishop of this, the oldest diocese on the American continent. It is a bit startling to American eyes to see, in the ground-floor of the episcopal palace, the offices of the National Lottery. The drawing takes place every Sunday, between mass and the bull-fight.

PARROTT RIFLED CANNON, ON THE SEA WALL,
PANAMA CITY.

Relic of American Civil War, usually mistaken for an old
Spanish gun.

Needless to say, there is much more taken in during the week from the many who buy tickets, than is paid out to the few who win prizes. This lottery is a shame and a curse to the Republic of Panama, but if our neighbors see fit to tolerate it, it is no affair of ours. Selling lottery-tickets or holding any such cruel sports as American Administration Building in background bull-fighting or cock-fighting, is strictly forbidden in the Canal Zone. The worst you can say of our Sundays there is that we let our wives and sisters go to church for us in the morning, and go ourselves to baseball games in the afternoon.

ATIONAL INSTITUTE OR, UNIVERSITY OF THE
REPUBLIC OF PANAMA.

The Panamanian Republican Band plays in the little park in the center of the Cathedral Plaza, every Sunday evening from eight to ten. Everybody from the President to the boot-black turns out in his best, to walk round and round the space in front of the bandstand and look at the pretty girls, or sit and sip iced drinks at a table outside one of the cafés, and criticize the music. Like all Latins, they are born musicians, those little brown bandsmen, and they play well.

But no music of theirs can stir an American's heart like that which he can hear at the camp of the Tenth United States Infantry at Empire, or of the Marines at Camp Elliott, when the men stand at attention as the flag comes slowly down, at the end of evening parade. Then you know what music means, when you hear a regimental band play "The Star-Spangled Banner," at sunset, down there in the jungle, two thousand miles from Home.

191

CHAPTER XV
HOW GENERAL GOETHALS HAS MADE GOOD

The task of building the Canal and governing the Canal Zone was placed, by an act of Congress in March, 1904, in the hands of the Isthmian Canal Commission, a board of seven men, appointed by the President, and responsible to him through the Secretary of War. Rear-Admiral John G. Walker, an officer on the retired list of the United States Navy, who had already been at the head of two earlier commissions appointed to study and compare the Panama and Nicaragua canal-routes, was made the chairman. Major-General George W. Davis was made the Governor of the Canal Zone. The other five members of the Commission were expert engineers, and, in July, John F. Wallace became the Chief Engineer.

The Walker Commission held office for a little more than a year. Under its leadership, law and order were firmly established in the Zone, many valuable surveys were made, a little dirt dug, the nucleus of an operating force collected, and the fight against fever begun by Dr. Gorgas. Under the circumstances, it was a very creditable year's work. For, instead of being given plenty of money and left undisturbed to organize its campaign against the jungle, the Isthmian Canal Commission was expected to make bricks, not only without straw, but almost without clay. Instead of realizing that millions of dollars' worth of machinery must be bought, the dirt and disease of four centuries scrubbed away, and a great army of men enlisted, drilled, housed, and fed, Congress could think of nothing but the danger of another scandal like that of the de Lesseps Company, and so doled out money in grudging driblets, while the American people kept crying, "Make the dirt fly!" with the same thoughtless impatience with which the people of the North cried, "On to Richmond!" before Bull Run. The Walker Commission gave it up in the spring of 1905.

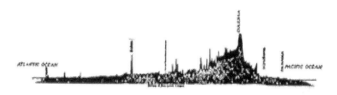

CROSS-SECTION OF THE ISTHMUS ON CANAL ROUTE.

The second Isthmian Canal Commission had for a chairman Mr. Theodore P. Shonts, a railroad president; but most of the active work was left to the Chief Engineer, Mr. John L. Stevens. To his skill as a practical, self-taught railroad-builder is due the scientific, labor-saving arrangement of the hundreds of miles of construction tracks over which the dirt-trains run to the dumps. Under Mr. Stevens—"Big Smoke Stevens" they called him, for he burned up cigars like Grant in the Wilderness—

the record for a month's excavation was brought up to a million cubic yards, the type of canal was finally settled on, and General Gorgas finished his fight against yellow fever. But in the spring of 1907, Mr. Shonts and Mr. Stevens both resigned.

Handling a large working force, especially one doing rough work in the open, is very much like commanding an army in the field. And an army commanded by a commission of seven men has exactly six generals too many. Realizing this, President Roosevelt decided to make the head of the third Isthmian Canal Commission not only its chairman, but also the Chief Engineer, the President of the Panama Railroad and the Governor of the Canal Zone. One man was made commander-in-chief; to stay there until he had finished the job. That man was Lieutenant-Colonel George Washington Goethals, United States Army Engineering Corps.

Born in Brooklyn, New York, June 29, 1858, of a family that had come from Holland to America only a few months before, he graduated second in his class from the United States Military Academy at West Point in 1880. This placed him among the honored few at the head of each class that are appointed to the engineering corps. Since then, General Goethals had spent his time in building locks, dams and irrigation ditches in the West, and coast-fortifications in the East, as instructor in engineering at West Point, chief engineer of the First Army Corps in the war with Spain, and as a member of the general staff in Washington, before he was sent to Panama.

The new commissioners were ordered to make their headquarters on the Isthmus and live there ten months in the year, instead of trying to dig the Canal from a comfortable office-building in Washington, D.C. There is no room here either for a full list of the many different commissioners— mostly officers of the engineering corps—who were appointed at this time or later, or for the barest outline of the good work that each has done. Colonel Sibert at Gatun, Colonel Gaillard in the Culebra Cut, Civil Engineer Rousseau, U.S.N., Colonel Hodges, Colonel Devol, and Mr. Williamson are among the many who have made their names honored on the Isthmus and among the fellow-members of their profession. But the man whose name will go down to history as the builder of the Panama Canal is General Goethals.

Soon after the General came to the Isthmus, an employee complained that almost no work was being done on his new house, although it was very far from completed, and he had been promised that it would be ready for his family in six weeks. Next morning General Goethals went there himself, and spoke to the carpenter-foreman in charge.

"You will have this house ready for use in six weeks."

"I'll try my best, sir, but—"

"That was not my order. You will have this house ready, for use, in six weeks. Do you understand?"

Six weeks later the family moved in.

This is General Goethal's way, both in big things and little. He goes to the spot, sees what is needed, gives a plain, direct order, and gets results instead of excuses. Every morning in the week he goes out on the line, not as his French predecessor did, in a private car drawn by a locomotive, but in a swift automobile mounted on flanged wheels, that looks like a taxicab disguised as a switch-engine. This motor-car is painted the regulation light yellow of Panama Railroad passenger-coaches, and you can scare a shirker out of a wet-season's growth by yelling, "Here comes the Yellow Peril!" But when the Yellow Peril—also known as the "Brain Wagon"—does come by, as likely as not it is empty; for the General frequently drops off to take a closer look at a steam-shovel, or a group of compressed-air drills, or a new drainage-ditch, or anything else that has attracted his interest. Presently he will come past, perched on top of a loaded dirt train, or walking at a good swinging pace over rough railroad ties and slippery fragments of splintered rock. In the afternoon he does his office work, and it is often late at night when he switches off the light over his desk.

THE BRAIN WAGON.
Also known as the "Yellow Peril" to the canal employees.

From a photograph, copyright, by Pach.
MAJOR-GENERAL GEORGE WASHINGTON
GOETHALS.

The time to see General Goethals at his best is on Sunday morning, when he sits in his dingy office at Culebra to give justice to all who come and ask for it. It is a scene as simple and as impressive as that of the good King Haroun-al-Raschid hearing his people's troubles, and judging between them, by the gate of Bagdad. Every man or woman who has a complaint of ill-treatment, or a suggestion for the improvement of the work, can walk in and tell it to the man at the top. Where else in the world could a laborer's wife, who is tired of getting tough meat from the butcher, say so to the head of a great business—a business so great that its monthly pay-roll is over $2,000,000—and have him not only listen to her courteously, but also attend to the matter himself?

General Goethals considers it part of his duty to make sixty-five thousand men, women and children satisfied with their houses, the furniture and plumbing therein, their food as supplied by the commissary or served at the hotels and messes, their washing as done by the government laundry, their amusements at the baseball parks, club-houses and band concerts, their chapels and lodges, the railroad and steamship service, the electric-light meters, the dentists, and even the icemen,—in the tropics at that. Everything, from the building and fortifying of the Canal, to explaining to Mrs. Jones why Mrs. Smith, whose husband gets twenty dollars less salary a month than hers, has received two more salt-cellars and an extra rocking-chair from the district quartermaster, rests on his shoulders, and he bears it all with a smile.

He watches and cares for his men as a trainer cares for his athletes, he has coached and drilled them till the forty thousand move together with the smooth team-play of a champion team; and he has breathed into the whole great organization the fighting spirit of its captain. He has proved himself a born fighter and leader of men, not by the number of lives he has taken—for he has never been to war—but by the battles he has won against the desert and the jungle. He has not worn his uniform since he came to Panama. But in spite of snow-white hair and civilian clothes, and more than thirty years' absence from the parade-ground, General Goethals is no shapeless, desk-chair warrior, but a man to inspire the words of Bret Harte's priest:

Now, by the firm grip of the hand on the bridle,
By the straight line from the heel to the shoulder,
By the curt speech,—nay, nay, no offense, son,—
You are a soldier.

President Lowell, of Harvard University, in conferring on General Goethals the honorary degree of doctor of laws, spoke of him as follows:

"George Washington Goethals, a soldier who has set a standard for the conduct of civic works; an administrator who has maintained security and order among a multitude of workmen in the tropics; an engineer who is completing the vast design of uniting two oceans through a peak in Darien."

STEAM SHOVEL LOADING FLAT CARS.

STEAM SHOVEL HANDLING A LARGE BOULDER.

CHAPTER XVI
WHAT THE FUTURE MAY BRING FORTH

January first, 1915, is the date set for the official opening of the Panama Canal. Unlike de Lesseps, who first announced positively that the Canal would be opened in a very short time, and then began to discover difficulties and make postponements, our engineers carefully studied the task before them, figured out that they could finish it by the first of June, 1914, and then added six months' extra time, to make sure. On the first of June, 1912, the excavation was more than seven-eighths completed, and the locks and dams were not far behind.

When asked if the Canal would not be opened ahead of schedule time, Colonel Goethals replied, "Some time in September, 1913, I expect to go over to Colon, take the Panama Railroad steamer that happens to be at the dock there, and put her through the Canal. If we get all the way across to the Pacific, I'll give it out to the newspapers, and if we don't, I'll keep quiet about it."

It is interesting to note that this first voyage of a ship across the American continent may take place four hundred years to a month, and perhaps to a day, after Balboa's discovery of the Pacific. Though the Canal will then be informally opened, a great deal more work will have to be done on it before it will be completely finished. The operating force will have to learn how to work the huge gates and elaborate sluices, and pilots must know how to take ships through the new waterway. To give them practice, as well as to accommodate commerce, vessels will be allowed to pass through the Canal during this period, at their owners' risk. The final test will be at the official opening, when a great fleet of American and foreign warships, led by the President of the United States in the *Mayflower*, and followed by a long line of yachts, excursion steamers, and merchant craft, will all pass through the Canal in procession. May the spirits of Columbus and Balboa be there to see!

But when we are done with the saluting and champagne-drinking, and speechifying (orators almost invariably refer to the Panama Canal as "mingling the waters of the two oceans," in spite of its having a high-level, fresh-water lake in the middle), what good is the Canal going to do us? What return are we going to get on the three hundred and fifty million dollars it hast cost us?

It is much easier to prophesy than to make your prophecies come true, as was proved in the case of the Suez Canal. Most people declared that it would be an utter failure, and instead it has made its stockholders rich; others thought it would restore the old commercial supremacy of the Mediterranean, but the people who most benefited by it were the English, who had taken no part in building it and made fun of the French for doing so; and finally, there were many unexpected results of the opening of the Suez Canal, that no one had dreamed of. For instance, it brought the Philippines so much nearer Spain that many more Spaniards went out there to make their fortunes, and they robbed the natives so energetically that the latter started a series of insurrections that did not end until after the islands became American. No man can tell what the ultimate results may be of the opening of the Panama Canal. But the benefits which we expect to derive from it may be divided into two classes: military and commercial.

Even if it should prove an utter failure commercially, the Canal would still be worth all it has cost us, for military purposes alone. Without it, Uncle Sam is in the position of a householder who has to run around the block to chase a tramp out of the back yard. With it, we can keep our navy concentrated in one powerful fleet, and move it from the Caribbean to San Francisco, or back again, in a couple of weeks. More than two months was required for the battle-ship *Oregon* to steam at full speed round South America from San Francisco to Cuba, where she was sorely needed at the outbreak of the Spanish-American War. Had the Panama Canal been in existence in 1898, she would have had to go only four thousand, six hundred miles, instead of thirteen thousand, four hundred, and she would have been ready to meet the enemy's fleet six weeks earlier—and a lot of things can happen in the first six weeks of a modern war.

To prevent any foreign fleet from capturing the Isthmus, and using the Canal against us, heavy fortifications are being built at both the Atlantic and Pacific ends. This work is being done by Lieutenant George R. Goethals. the elder son of the builder of the Canal. More than twelve million dollars is to be spent in building great concrete forts and gun-pits on the islands and headlands, and arming them with batteries of twelve-inch mortars and fourteen-inch disappearing-guns. Most formidable of all will be the gigantic sixteen-inch gun, now at Sandy Hook, that can throw a shell, capable of sinking the stoutest dreadnaught, for more than twenty miles. Without these forts to keep them at a respectful distance, a few blockading vessels would have our fleet at their mercy as it came down the narrow channel in single column, or they might bombard the locks at Miraflores or Gatun. But modern battle-ships are too costly to be risked in a direct attack on coast-fortifications, which are usually captured by landing an army at some other point, and attacking the forts from the landward side, as at Port Arthur. For that reason, a permanent garrison is to be kept in the Canal Zone, of a brigade of infantry, a squadron of cavalry, and a battalion of field artillery, besides the gunners in the forts.

Every lock will be defended by earthworks against an attack overland. The operating machinery will be safely stowed inside the square center-pier (see diagram on page 182), beneath a thick concrete ceiling that should protect it from any bombs dropped from hostile aëroplanes. (It would be much easier for our soldiers to launch their own aëroplanes from a parade-ground or the broad top of a lock-wall, than for an attacking force to launch theirs from the deck of a ship.) The Gatun Dam is so thick and the lock-gates so many that there is very little danger of any one's blowing them all up and letting the water out of the lake. To keep spies from dynamiting the gates, the locks will be lighted by electricity at night, and guarded at all times by sentries. In case of an attack on the lock-guard by a strong body of men, reinforcements could be quickly brought, by road, rail, or water, from the central camp at Culebra. Here the main body of the garrison is to be encamped, across the Canal from the present town of Culebra, which, together with nearly all the rest of the settlements in the Canal Zone, is to be abandoned, both because of the relocation of the railroad, and for military reasons. The entire country will be allowed to grow up again into thick jungle, through which no civilized army, encumbered with horses and cannon, could cut a path without giving our men plenty of time and warning to prepare a very warm reception.

A PAIR OF GATES, GATUN LOCKS.

View taken in August, 1911, looking North toward the Atlantic entrance. This shows the construction of the upper lock, with the east wall of the upper, middle, amd lower locks in the distance.

It is a strange and melancholy fact that we in the twentieth century should deliberately let our borders grow up into forests to keep our neighbors at a distance, even as our barbarous German ancestors did, two thousand years ago. Some day humanity may become sufficiently civilized to establish universal peace. But until then, we must not forget that Panama has always been seized and held by the strong hand. The Isthmus today is a thousand times richer and more tempting a prize than it was in the time of Drake or Morgan, and though piracy has gone out of fashion, war has not. When we can turn the regular army into a police force, sell the navy for old iron, and take the big guns from Sandy Hook and the Golden Gate, we can leave the Panama Canal to be protected by the Zone Police,—but not before then. So much for the military side; now for the commercial.

A model town of concrete houses is to be built at Balboa for the operating force. Here will be the offices of the permanent Canal headquarters, and barracks for a battalion of marines, who may be needed to keep drunken stevedores and sailors from breaking up the toy police force of Panama City. An anchorage basin is being dredged and lined with an elaborate system of concrete docks, and the hundreds of acres of new land that have been made by filling in tidal swamps with earth and rock from Gaillard Cut will some day be covered with warehouses, that should pay a very profitable rental to Uncle Sam. Electricity for lighting the streets, heating the electric stoves in the houses, and operating the cargo-cranes and other machinery, will be supplied by the spillway power-plant at Gatun (see page 174). Here at Balboa will be concentrated the present machine-shops, the commissary with its cold-storage plant and bakery, and the Government laundry, which now plans to take the soiled linen from a ship at one end of the Canal, and send it back clean, via the Panama Railroad, before the vessel reaches the other side of the Isthmus. What with these, and the handy tanks and pipe-line of the Union Oil Company of California, and his own dry-docks, coal-bunkers, and barges, Uncle Sam will be able to supply every ship going through the Canal with anything from a sea-biscuit to a new propeller-shaft. Not only will these superior accommodations attract commerce to Panama that would otherwise go to Suez, but some day this peaceful, profitable trade may be worth more to us than money can tell, when a fleet of transports comes hurrying through with empty bunkers, or a battered dreadnaught limps into Balboa shipyards, to be sent back to the fighting line. Professor Emory R. Johnson, Special Commissioner on Panama Canal Traffic and Tolls, says, in his report to the Secretary of War:

"The distance from New York to San Francisco, by way of the Straits of Magellan, is 13,135 nautical miles, by way of Panama, 5,262 miles, the Canal route being 7,873 miles shorter. The saving between New Orleans and San Francisco is greater—8,868 nautical miles—the Magellan route being longer and the Canal route shorter from New Orleans than from New York. The Canal will reduce the distance from New York to the Chilian nitrate port, Iquique, 5,139 nautical miles, to Valparaiso 3,747 miles, to Coronel 3,296, and Valdivia about 2,900 miles. For New Orleans and other Gulf ports, the reduction is greater." It is only 1,395 miles from New Orleans to Colon, while from New York to Colon it is 1,974 miles.

The Pacific coast of the United States is the region that expects to be most immediately benefited, and for that reason the Panama Pacific Exposition is to be held in San Francisco in 1915. California oranges and lemons and Oregon apples can be shipped much more cheaply in refrigerator-ships than in refrigerator-cars, while the saving on wheat, coal, lumber, and other heavy freight is even greater.

Most of the passenger traffic will still go by rail, as an express train can go from New York to San Francisco in four days, while the fastest steamer would take two weeks. But many of the emigrants from Europe, that now crowd into the tenements of New York, will probably sail through the Canal directly to the Pacific coast, where there is only too much room for them.

On the Atlantic coast, New Orleans plans to combine the traffic through the Canal with a great revival of the Mississippi River trade, while every port from Boston to Galveston claims to be in the most direct path to Panama and to have the best railroad facilities behind it. Over a hundred million dollars is being spent on each coast in dredging channels, building docks, and otherwise getting ready for Panama. The effects should be felt, in lower freight rates and prices, in the farthest inland parts of the United States.

The Panama Canal will bring our Atlantic and Gulf coasts, and the whole Mississippi Valley much nearer China, Australia, and New Zealand, all hungry for American steel and coal and manufactured goods. Then there is the trade with South America, which proved so much more valuable than that of the west coast of North America, in the early days of the Panama Railroad. But though the South Americans like our reapers and binders and other machinery, and are beginning to wear our ready-made clothes and shoes, they do not like our stupid, bad-mannered ways of doing business with them. We send them circulars and catalogues written in a language they cannot read, salesmen who cannot speak a word of Spanish, and goods packed in flimsy cases that usually go to pieces on the voyage. If an American schoolboy or office-boy, who is thinking of becoming a salesman, were to spend some of his time studying the Spanish language (or Portuguese, for Brazil), and learning something of the history, customs, etiquette (good manners sell more goods than "hustle," in the tropics) of the other republics in this hemisphere, he would be giving himself some of the training that the English and German salesmen are put through before they are sent to South or Central America, where they have built up an immensely profitable trade. A generation ago, Horace Greeley said, "Go West, young man, go West!" To-morrow the word may be, "Go South!"

BUILDING PEDRO MIGUEL LOCKS

Eventually, the Panama Canal may help restore the long-lost American merchant marine. At the outbreak of the War of 1812, more than ninety per cent, of American goods were carried in American ships; in 1912, we paid a freight bill of over two billion dollars to foreign shipowners. At the outbreak of the Civil War, we had the greatest merchant marine in the world; fifty years later, we had less than a dozen ships trading to foreign ports. This was due partly to the replacing of wooden sailing vessels with steel steamers, but more to our faulty navigation laws,—for steel can be made in Pittsburg more cheaply than anywhere else in the world. All the big European and Japanese liners are subsidized, or partly paid for, by the governments of their countries, who use them to carry the mails in time of peace, and for cruisers or troop-ships in time of war. If a great war should break out in Europe or Asia, many of these vessels would cease to come to our ports, and we should have a hard time doing business with the rest of the world. And if we went to war ourselves, our army and navy would be crippled for want of transports and colliers. When we sent our battle-ship fleet around the world in 1907, its coal and provisions had to be carried in foreign ships, that would not be permitted to serve it in time of war.

Yet today, when the Stars and Stripes are almost never seen on the high seas, except on a warship or a private yacht, we have more sailing vessels than any other country in the world. England, of course, has the greatest numbers of steamers, but who do

211

you suppose has the second greatest? Neither Germany nor Japan, but the United States. That is because of the ships on the Great Lakes, and in the coastwise trade. Only American vessels are allowed to go from one American port to another. For that reason, American ships plying between our two coasts will pass through the Panama Canal without paying any tolls. The same will be true of all mail steamers, subsidized by the United States Government and liable for use in case of war.

Otherwise, the Canal is to be for the peaceful use of all nations, without favoritism. A uniform toll of a dollar and a quarter a ton is to be charged on all ships passing through, whatever flag they sail under. As most of the European governments have been in the habit of paying the tolls at Suez on liners belonging to their subjects, they will probably do the same at Panama. Without some such assistance, American shipowners will probably find it more profitable to stick to the trade between our two coasts—and those of Mexico and Central America on the way—without venturing to South America and the Far East, where a hundred years ago the sea was white with the tall sails of the Yankee clippers.

What effect will the opening of the Canal have on the Republic of Panama? The money spent there during the years when it was being built has brought great prosperity to the Isthmus, but that source of revenue will soon come to an end. It would not be surprising if a period of "hard times" were to follow, for that was what happened as soon as the Panama Railroad was finished in 1855, and travelers began to cross the Isthmus in a few hours instead of a week. Undoubtedly most of the traffic will pass through the Canal without breaking bulk, and the Panamanian merchants will have Uncle Sam to compete with in the sale of everything but picture postcards and souvenirs to tourists. But Panama has an excellent chance to become prosperous, by supplying the ships that pass through with fresh beef, fruit, and vegetables. On the broad, fertile prairies of the Province of Chiriqui (between the Canal Zone and Costa Rica), there is the best of grazing for cattle, while everything can be grown there, from bananas and oranges at the sea-level, to apples and other northern fruit in the hills. The United Fruit Company is doing a great trade at the Atlantic port of Bocas del Toro, and many Americans are beginning to settle near David, the capital of the province.

Though it has an area as big as the State of New York, with its twelve million inhabitants, the Republic of Panama has a population of only three hundred and fifty thousand. Most of these are negroes, with a slight admixture of Indian blood, being the descendants of the Spanish slaves or workmen on the railroad or the Canal. Nearly all the white blood, as well as most of the wealth and business of the country, is concentrated in a small aristocracy, sometimes called the "Ten Families." If Chiriqui should begin to fill up with American farmers and cattlemen, a situation would be created very much like that in Texas in the early part of the nineteenth century, requiring the greatest tact on the part of the United States Government.

Across the Canal Zone, at the South American end of the Republic, things are very much today as they were four hundred years ago, in what was then called Darien, and is now spoken of as "the San Blas country." Here, as in the heart of the Florida Everglades, and in certain parts of South America, the red man is still supreme. He does not bother us in the Canal Zone, and we do not bother him. He is well supplied with the white man's weapons. Masters of trading-schooners that have plied up and down the San Blas coast for thirty years have seen from their decks rich stretches of hardwood jungle and fertile prairie, and have noticed the heavy gold ornaments worn by the Indians who paddled out to barter with them; but the traders have not gone ashore to investigate. No white man or negro may set foot in the San Blas country after sunset under penalty of death, by tribal law. When President Mendoza of the Republic of Panama went up the coast in a United States Government tug in 1908, he saw the Colombian flag flying above an Indian village some miles on his side of the Panama-Colombian border, and the Indians would not let him land even to protest to their chief about it. The San Blas have no use for white men: there is not a missionary, or a trader, or a half-breed in their country, and no white man has ever gone through it from Panama to South America. Miss Annie Coop, an American missionary, visited the San Blas country for a short time in 1909, and hopes to be permitted to return there soon and establish a school, for while the tribal law excludes white men, it says nothing about white women. But neither the strictest tribal law nor the bravest tribal warriors, have ever kept white men permanently out of a country where there was gold. Sooner or later, there will be another "gold-rush"; a stampede of white men across this last frontier, outrages, treachery, and massacres on both sides, which the feeble Republic of Panama will be powerless to prevent, and which may force the armed intervention of the United States. Let us hope this may never come to pass. But it is not easy to keep white men on one side of a border, when there is gold on the other. As they were before Columbus came, so the Darien Indians are today, within fifty miles of where we are living in electric-lighted houses, and building the Panama Canal.

A LIGHTHOUSE IN THE JUNGLE

Soon the work will be finished and the long task done. Then the great working force will be broken up and scattered to the four corners of the earth, and the jungle will creep back and swallow up their houses as it has those of the Spaniards and the Frenchmen before them. But every American who has worked more than two years on the Canal will carry away with him, besides imperishable memories of the biggest, cleanest job the world has ever seen, the medal you see reproduced on this page. It is made of bronze from one of the dredges abandoned by the de Lesseps Company, as the Victoria Cross is made of the bronze of captured cannon; and like it, it is given for brave and arduous service. The design, chosen by the canal-builders themselves, shows on one side the head of Theodore Roosevelt; on the other, a picture of the finished canal. Beneath is set the seal of the Canal Zone, a noble galleon, sailing full-fraught through the long-sought passage to the Indies; and above the motto from that seal, "The land divided—the world united."

THE PANAMA CANAL MEDAL.

GENERAL VIEW OF GATUN LOCKS.
Showing bulkhead to keep water of sea level canal out of the
lock-chamber
during erection of the gates.

COLLAPSIBLE STEEL FORM FOR CASTING CULVERT
IN LOCK WALL.

CHAPTER XVII
THE OPENING OF THE CANAL

Water was first turned into the Gatun Locks on September 26, 1913. Several thousand canal employees lined the lock walls to watch the muddy fountains spurt up out of the round openings in the dusty concrete floors of the lock chambers. With the water came hundreds of big bull-frogs, sucked down through the sluices from the lake above, who swam round and round in comic bewilderment as the water-line rose higher and higher. When the water in the lowest lock was even with the surface of the sea-level canal outside, the gates were opened and the sea-going tug *Gatun* steamed in under her own power, for the electric towing-locomotives were not yet ready for service. General Goethals was not a passenger on the tug; but walked up and down the lock wall, receiving reports on how the valves and bull-wheels were working, and watching the *Gatun* as she was locked through to the lake

Two weeks later, on October 10, President Wilson pressed a button in the White House, and started an electric impulse which was relayed southward from cable-station to cable-station till it reached and exploded eight tons of dynamite, blowing up the Gamboa Dike and admitting the water of Gatun Lake into the Gaillard Cut. The Cut had already been partially flooded, that the inrush of water might not be too severe. About twenty minutes after the dike was blown up, two daredevil young Americans in a dugout "shot the rapids" from the lake into the Cut. One of these young men was a private in the Marine Corps; the other was Lindon Bates, Jr., who was killed while trying to save some children on board the *Lusitania*.

THE DREDGING FLEET AT CUCARACHA.

But after the last man-made dike had been cleared away, the Canal was still closed to navigation by a great natural barrier. This was our old friend, the Cucaracha Slide, which had slid down and almost completely blocked the bottom of the Cut in January, 1913. So little impression had the steam shovels been able to make on it in the next nine months that it was decided to turn in the water and finish the job with floating dredges. A

219

small fleet of ladder- and dipper-dredges were brought up from the Atlantic entrance, while up through Miraflores and Pedro Miguel locks came the most powerful dredge in the world, the *Corozal*, with her endless chain of buckets that can bring up ten thousand tons a day, and dig through soft rock without previous blasting. This vessel was built at Renfrew, Scotland, and made the voyage across the Atlantic and round South America to the Pacific entrance of the Canal under her own steam.

Moored as closely together as possible, the dredges attacked the great mass of soft clay from both sides. Double crews and electric light enabled the work to go on by night as well as by day. The excavated material was loaded into barges, towed away by tugs, and dumped into Gatun or Miraflores Lake, outside the ship channel.

By May, 1914, a channel had been dug through the Cucaracha Slide deep enough to permit barges to be towed through from ocean to ocean. These barges carried freight from steamers of the American-Hawaiian Steamship Line, which company had been prevented from trans-shipping by the Tehuantepec Railroad because of the revolutionary outbreaks in Mexico.

After the dredges had removed 2,767,080 cubic yards—an average of 286,239.78 cubic yards per month—from the Cucaracha Slide, its forward movement ceased and the Way was opened for an ocean-going ship to make the long-looked-forward-to passage from sea to sea. This trip was made by the *Cristobal*, of the Panama Railroad Steamship

Line, on August 3, 1914. Her sister ship, the *Ancon*, passed through on the fifteenth, carrying a large party of army officers, Panamanian dignitaries, and their wives and families. Again General Goethals was not a passenger, but watched the vessel's passage from the shore, moving from point to point in his railroad motor.

The Panama Canal was now declared open to the commerce of the world. During the first twelve months there passed through it 1258 vessels, carrying 5,675,261 tons of cargo, the tolls on which amounted to $4,909,150.96.

U.S.S. *OHIO* PASSING CUCARACHA SLIDE, JULY 16, 1915.

The Isthmian Canal Commission was abolished on January 27, 1914. Two days later, President Wilson nominated Colonel Goethals first Governor of the Panama Canal. This appointment was speedily and unanimously confirmed by the Senate, and on March 4, 1915, the Governor was promoted to his present rank of Major-General.

But his work was not yet done at Panama. In October, 1915, the Canal was completely blocked by two formidable slides directly opposite each other on the banks of the Cut, a little distance north of Gold Hill. Both of these slides were of the type known as "breaks," where the weight of the bank causes the underlying material to snap off and give way like an overloaded floor-beam. In each of these cases, about eighty acres of ground sank almost straight down to an average depth of twenty feet. Squeezed between its sinking banks, the bottom of the Canal naturally rose up, forming first an island, then a peninsula, and finally a complete barrier. As fast as the dredges dug this away, more material came down from each side, in regular waves. The tops of these slides were too broken to permit of their being lightened by steam-shovels, nor could anything be done by washing the earth down the side of the slope away from the Cut, with powerful hydraulic nozzles, as was possible at Cucaracha. The only course was to keep the dredges digging away, till there was nothing more left for them to dig. It was not until April, 1916, that the Canal was reopened to commerce.

PEDRO MIGUEL LOCKS.
Vessel in East Chamber going north, and one in West
Chamber going south.

Because of these slides and also because of the great war in Europe, which made impossible the assembling of an international fleet, there was no formal opening of the Panama Canal by the President of the United States. In somewhat the same way, the elaborate festivities in celebration of the opening of the Suez Canal were cut short forty-five years earlier, by the outbreak of the Franco-Prussian War.

Made in the USA
Middletown, DE
12 December 2017